The
Southern Way

The regular volume for the Southern devotee

Kevin Robertson

Issue 43

DOVER MARINE

www.crecy.co.uk

© 2018 Crécy Publishing Ltd
and the various contributors

ISBN 9781909328778

First published in 2018 by Noodle Books
an imprint of Crécy Publishing Ltd

All editorial submissions to:
The Southern Way (Kevin Robertson)
Conway
Warnford Rd
Corhampton
Hants SO32 3ND
Tel: 01489 877880
editorial@thesouthernway.co.uk

A CIP record for this book is available from the British Library

Publisher's note: Every effort has been made to identify and correctly attribute photographic credits. Any error that may have occurred is entirely unintentional.
In line with the new design the front cover image has changed from that originally advertised. All other information is unaffected.

Printed in England by LatimerTrend

Noodle Books is an imprint of
Crécy Publishing Limited
1a Ringway Trading Estate
Shadowmoss Road
Manchester M22 5LH

www.crecy.co.uk

Front cover:
The ubiquitous 'Terrier' and likely no prizes for guessing this is the Hayling Island branch as well. Considering the traffic chaos that ensues accessing Hayling Island by road at peak times – well most of the time really – it is a great pity this railway did not survive. But the 'Terriers' could hardly have been expected to last into the twenty-first century even if we might have wished it. Instead we got the excuse of the age of the only available motive power and the condition of the wooden bridge at Langstone Harbour that were both too expensive to replace, even if it was admitted the railway was making a small profit. Memories then of a scene not replicated here since November 1963. 'Terrier' No 32650 survived the closure of the line, just, well on paper at least, but was withdrawn from Eastleigh on 20 November 1963 along with the remaining four members of the class, now redundant and no longer needed for branch line services. As No 50 it is now preserved on the Spa Valley Railway.

Rear cover:
Another one with no prizes for guessing the location, Axminster, of course, but taken from a less usual angle with the branch train leaving the bay platform – but just look at what is passing alongside! A fine view of No 30582 in the evening sun with its two-coach train to Lyme Regis. But oh for more of the tavern car set running alongside on the up main. The sign can just be made out but I doubt well enough to be identified; lovely early BR livery as well, if only for a bit more… No 30582 appears to have suffered some loss of paint from below the smokebox as well, probably hot ashes.

Title page:
A pair of MLVs (Motor Luggage Vans) at an easily recognisable location. Unfortunately it is not possible to identify their running numbers. The '75' headcode refers to a Victoria-Dover Marine service running via the Catford Loop and Chatham. Ten of the type were built at Eastleigh between 1951 and 1961 intended as additional luggage accommodation on boat trains running on the Eastern Section. It was the days when a passenger might be accompanied by numerous trunks and cases. Originally numbered 68001-10, they were variously renumbered until in their final days they became Nos 9001-10. Aside from being able to operate on 750v DC third rail, the vehicles also had batteries allowing up to thirty minutes' traction at low speed on non-electrified lines. The batteries were recharged when the vehicle was again taking power from the third rail. When operating with the CEP units on the South Eastern section it was thus common to see thirteen-coach trains: three x 4-CEP (or similar) and an MLV. Consequent upon the closure of Dover Western Docks station and the end of specific boat train services, all were withdrawn in 1991–92. After this the series were transferred to departmental service as tractor units, with several finding a new role as depot shunters. In this final role they remained at work, with two exceptions, until 1997–98. The first exception was No 68006, which was withdrawn in 1991 having sustained collision damage, whilst at the opposite end of the scale, No 68002 was retained by South West Trains until at late as 2004. Eight of the original ten were saved for preservation at various sites, the exceptions being No 68006 already mentioned, and 68007, which despite passing into preservation was scrapped for spares in 2006.

Contents

Issue No 44 of THE SOUTHERN WAY
ISBN 9781909328761
available in October 2018 at £14.95

To receive your copy the moment it is released, order in advance from your usual supplier, or it can be sent post-free (UK) direct from the publisher:

Crécy Publishing Ltd

1a Ringway Trading Estate, Shadowmoss Road, Manchester M22 5LH

Tel 0161 499 0024

www.crecy.co.uk

enquiries@crecy.co.uk

Introduction

I take as my theme for this issue the topic of photographs – railway that is – and the use thereof (referring to Southern primarily, of course), but the same would apply to any railway image.

In bleakest February (well bleak so far as England is concerned with just a few snowdrops likely wishing they had stayed within their bulbs rather than venturing outwards) I received an email from *SW* friend Nigel Barnes-Evans. Now Nigel is a man I have known for, well, shall we say, a few years, going back to a time when we were both 'better thatched' on top. He is also a regular provider of material, although I am ashamed to admit, probably too little has appeared under his actual name. Nigel regularly sends in pieces he has picked up at exhibitions and shows, and in the case of photographs often with nothing written on the reverse to indicate location, date, etc., or even ownership. Such was the case with his latest offering.

This got me thinking: images you have personally taken will be known by you, not all the details perhaps, but likely most. So an immediate plea, please do add some notes to the rear of prints – it can help a lot and this is regardless of subject; domestic or hobby/interest. I say this as we will all have an intimate knowledge of our own 'patch' but others may not, and as collections and individual prints are becoming ever more widely spread this can become a genuine problem, especially with railway views when there might literally be nothing but open track and country to be seen.

Which in turn set me thinking further: just now many railway photographs might have been taken over the years? Thousands certainly; tens of thousands, yes again; hundreds of thousands, again yes; millions and I suspect we are getting closer.

To justify this estimate, first think of the official photographs taken by the railway companies themselves, mostly now residing with the NRM. Then there are the renowned individuals working either pre-war or between and after wartime whose images might have become part of the LG.R.P, Real Photographs group. Next are the respected and prolific photographers such as Dr Ian C. Allan, R.C. Riley, S.C. Nash, etc. – there are literally hundreds of such names. Come post-war and with something like 300,000 members of the Ian Allan Locospotters club at its peak we can likely conclude that a fair number of these also had a camera at some stage even if, and as I was mentioning earlier, they may not have ventured far off their 'own turf' or even produced little more than snapshots.

As if to prove this number we only have to look at the vast number of photographs that are available from locations such as ColourRail, Transport Treasury, the NRM, Rail Archive Stephenson, Alan Sainty, Messrs Blencowe, Lens of Sutton, etc. (other well respected collections are also available!) plus nowadays with the advent of the internet, where collections or odd images can quickly be placed for the benefit of a wider audience. Add all these together and it can easily be seen how the total can add up to a seven, eight or an even larger figure. So if you ask the obvious, 'Was a photograph ever taken of...?', the answer is likely 'yes', albeit it is probably the same as most others as it would appear many were content to stand in a similar position to their neighbour. Again without stating the obvious, if you are looking, say, for a photograph of No 35030 at Basingstoke, with luck you will probably find it. But go back in time fifty years and look for, say, T9 No 119 in the same location and the rule of diminishing returns applies. Subjects other than locomotives can also be more problematical to find.

So finding your sought-after image is relatively easy (someone will come back and bite me I am sure on this) but with this also comes a problem – ownership. Suppose you now want to use it to illustrate an article? Can you, should you? If it has been obtained from a reputable source, you ask permission and all should be well, but what happens if that is not the case? *Caveat emptor* and all that.

Now I am NOT a solicitor and I am not going to attempt to pontificate on the laws of copyright in any way. Instead I will just mention some of the likely pitfalls:

1 You have purchased a print but who owns the copyright?

2 What happens if two or more places are selling copies of the same image, each claiming the rights?

3 What if there is no indication of ownership written on the reverse?

4 What if the original copyright holder whose name does appear on the reverse has passed on the rights to another party? Perhaps you had permission originally but how would/could you know the rights have altered, especially if your own consent was originally just by word of mouth?

5 How do you attempt to trace ownership?

The list is likely endless.

I say all this because *Southern Way*, and no doubt many other specialist journals, rely upon imagery to work. We are not into the tens of thousands as regards circulation – I wish we were but realistically never will be – whilst a journal without pictures would probably have limited appeal. We therefore deliberately include a genuine rider along the lines, 'We welcome articles but contributors must have permission to reproduce images'; the same could be said about articles as well. Not many people will likely write a piece on 'Working with the Q1s at night' (flippant title) but if somebody else did, how does the editor know that it is not plagiarism? We simply cannot have eyes everywhere.

It was this view from Nigel Barnes-Evans that started me on this particular soapbox. Too interesting to ignore yet posing any number of questions. First, what we know: T9 No 30117 with a down special at Millbrook. The line on the extreme right is the Fawley branch, so No 30117 is heading west. The print is on that horrible matt paper with a silvery tint, hence the minute dots are not dust. No date, no name, no details, indeed it took some time to even identify the location with some other suggestions being close to Lymington Junction. We also know it is a Special working of some sort: 'SPL 11' on the lower disc, and Bournemouth line code: six horseboxes, seemingly nine cattle wagons and a utility brake at the rear. (The seeming embellishment between the chimney and dome is the head of a colour light signal applicable to the other, up, line.) Trying now to determine more, No 30117 was variously at either Salisbury or Eastleigh from 1948 until its end in 1961. A local working perhaps, or a train taken over by the T9 at some stage? Turning to the stock, empty or loaded, again we cannot know. What is suggested are empty vehicles to perhaps Beaulieu Road for New Forest ponies – but so many, or was it even a mixture of loads for different destinations? Could it be for the regular hunts held at Dorchester, or simplest of all, some form of farm removal train? With a date it should be possible to ascertain more, proving the point again of the importance of recording information. Whatever, Nigel thank you; perhaps someone will come back with more.

I have fallen foul of copyright once. It was an altogether unpleasant affair that occurred some years ago and it still hurts, especially as it was a genuine mistake and the other party appeared to deliberately set out to be as nasty as possible. I have heard other similar tales as well. And yes, it was a railway book, the complainant a name well known at the time. It goes to prove not everyone in our hobby is as pleasant as we might wish. I have also seen images that I know I have personally found in the course of research, blatantly copied and used in other publications or on the net. Mostly I will not seek redress – live and let live I hope – as yours truly will also get it wrong sometimes.

We live in a litigation-strewn world; one word out of place or remark made and it seems the word 'sue' is the next thing said. I am even told that recently one large UK publisher has written to all its authors asking, nay insisting, that every illustration they intend to use in any book being submitted must be accompanied by written clearance from the copyright holder. In our type of market I would suggest this is almost impossible. But as we said

before, how do we always know who that copyright holder might be? (My comments do not refer to a specific railway publisher, although the firm concerned is a household name, but clearly it is somebody who has had their fingers burned.)

So to return to the start. Do I therefore reject Nigel's submitted images, do I insist upon written clearance, how do I know they are not illicit copies? The short answer is I trust Nigel implicitly and elsewhere still rely on good old-fashioned British honesty and integrity. If we make a mistake – sorry, it happens. We will genuinely try not to let it happen again. So please do continue to submit your articles and images, if they can be checked for permission so much the better, otherwise please advise in advance – we may even have contact details of some of the owners ourselves. I hope the results that appear in *SW*, and of course the veritable plethora of other journals and books, will continue to delight and feed our enthusiasm.

Kevin Robertson

The Southern Railway and the Imperial Airways Traffic

For our lead article in this issue we are privileged to be able to reproduce a copy of the late D.W. (Derek) Winkworth's piece on the Southern Railway and Imperial Airways traffic. A copy of the original work was passed to us by Tony Teague, who together with Mike Radford made the suggestion we include it in *SW*. An article on the same subject by Derek Winkworth first appeared in the 2000 publication, *Southern Special Traffic* by Irwell Press but is now long out of print. We feel then the time is right for a revisit of this fascinating topic and with a number of additions.

Of all special traffic operations that the newly formed Southern Railway might be expected to become involved with, perhaps the most unlikely would be air passenger movements. In the mid-1920s, just at the time the SR was finding its feet, Imperial Airways (IA) was in turn discovering its wings much in the same way as the railway company – both being a grouping of companies – although the former trailed the railway by fifteen months with its own formation in April 1924. (Imperial was formed from the British Marine Air Navigation Company Ltd, the Daimler Airway, Handley Page Transport Ltd and the Instone Air Line Ltd.)

Possibly with an eye to winning over the four railway companies as allies rather than having them as competitors, as well as safeguarding his own company's position, the chairman of Imperial Airways, Sir Eric Geddes, wrote to all four railways on 9 July 1929 suggesting a meeting with each to seek areas where IA might co-operate. This undoubtedly had been prompted by the granting that year of powers to the railways to operate air services within certain limits, as the opening sentence, 'Now that you have got your Air Powers...' of Sir Eric's letters acknowledged.

To Sir Herbert Walker, the Southern's general manager, Sir Eric wrote, 'The chief advantage which we could see at the present time would be if Victoria Station were to be a starting point for

Slightly later in history but worthy of inclusion is this view of Westland Wessex three-engine monoplane G-AAGW, the first aircraft acquired by the GWR but dating from April 1929. It operated out of Castle Bromwich, then the airport for Birmingham, and was used on various routes including the fifty-minute trip to Croydon airport. (Even in those days it was reported the time taken from city centre to airport added between one and two hours to the journey.) It subsequently went to Air Pilot Training and ended its days in 1964. G-AAGW is seen here at Castle Bromwich likely c.1933. *The Wallis collection*

air travel and until such time as it justifies a SR station at Croydon Aerodrome we would appreciate being able to start our passengers at Victoria Station … might like to start the association at Victoria in anticipation of that day.' On 26 July a 'little discussion was held on operating a fast train service between Victoria and Croydon aerodrome' and it was agreed that it was a matter in which the Air Ministry would have to be consulted.

Reaction of the railway companies to Sir Eric's approach varied from seeming inertia on the part of Wedgwood from the LNER through opportunism by Milne of the GWR to the foresight of Walker of the Southern. (Surprisingly the LMS is not mentioned.) Walker recognised that air services probably posed the railways their greatest threat, insofar as the SR was concerned by drawing off traffic to the Continent, but intended to keep matters at arm's length until it could be seen how things would develop. Meanwhile, a memorandum (as it was to be known) was agreed between IA and the SR whereby IA undertook to operate services on charter to the SR and the SR agreed to charter all its air services from IA; such services not to be in direct competition with IA services. Notwithstanding what was a six-year timespan since the formation of Imperial Airways, this memorandum was not entered into until February 1930, just at the time of the trade slump and seemingly with little immediate likelihood of anything much resulting therefrom.

The first time the public was to be made aware of the interest of railways in air services was in April 1933 when the Great Western Railway stole the show by starting a Cardiff-Haldon (Teignmouth) service with a Westland Wessex aircraft painted in chocolate and cream (what else!) on charter from and staffed by IA. This was following advice from H. Burchall (IA) to C.B. Collett (GWR) on 27 March 1933 and considered to be the best proposition to inaugurate air services operated by the GWR.

The year 1934 saw the formation of the Railway Air Services, with the SR a rather unwilling partner as its board viewed the RAS agreement still with the suspicion that it would abstract Continental traffic from the railway. Walker was also obliged to terminate the 1930 memorandum with IA because it was inconsistent with the RAS arrangement, which he did on 2 June 1934.

Meanwhile, an initiative by IA in 1933 had led to the Government agreeing to the proposal that the company should carry all first class letter mail from the United Kingdom to Empire destinations by air without surcharge. The Empire Air Mail Scheme (EAMS) had been born: IA was to provide aircraft and servicing facilities and undertake operation from airports provided by others. A glance at an atlas of the 1930s quickly showed that most parts of the Empire could offer waterside facilities either in sea or lake form as accommodation for flying boats, which would avoid constructing airport runways, and this was possibly as large a factor as any in deciding that a squadron of flying-boats – the famous 'C' class – should be built for the service. Thus, in October 1934 the search for a site not more than one hour's train journey from London began, ranging from anywhere in Kent, Sussex and Hampshire as far as Southampton – although how it was considered that everywhere in this sector could be reached within the hour was not elaborated upon!

At the same time IA set about finding the site for a London terminal, although it does not require a lot of insight to discover that Victoria was always in mind, possibly because an IA office had already been established at 130 Wilton Road, Victoria on a lease from the SR. An internal IA memo from Secretary to Chairman of 4 February 1935 included such points as:

(a) The Southern Railway to allow us to build a suitable departure station over their tracks near Victoria with proper access to the railway departure station and to a private siding.

(b) To operate for us our own special trains at the highest possible speeds between Victoria and the airport we eventually obtain for our Empire services.

(c) The Southern Railway to use all their powers to construct such extensions to their lines as may be necessary to enable our special trains to be run into our airport.

Investigations of London terminal sites by IA resulted in comments such as: 'Charing Cross station – congested, cannot extend; Waterloo station – not attractive site; Holborn Viaduct – congested; Hudson's Repository, Victoria – not on the market; Pullman Car Company's site Victoria station – too small; LPTB site Victoria – costly and no direct access to railway; Victoria station – favourable. The Southern Railway guarantee a quick service from platform 17 to any Empire Airport which might be chosen at any of the following: anywhere along the Thames reaches East of Central London, Grain, Lympne, Portsmouth, and Southampton.'

To further Victoria, in March 1935 the SR supplied IA with a layout of Victoria station and stated that Grain or Langston would be suitable for operating services to but that Southampton might be difficult.

The suggestion that Waterloo might be easier and thus could be used as the London terminus for Southampton (and presumably Langston) did not find favour with IA, which seemed to have a fixation of having a terminal in Buckingham Palace Road complete with a suitable tower that could be seen by an observer at the west end of The Mall. Apparently this 'observer person' should have been suitably impressed by viewing Admiralty Arch in one direction and the IA Terminal Tower in the other – perceived as outward and visible manifestations of sea and air power.

IA got their lease of land in Buckingham Palace Road from the SR so that the London terminal site was assured and work could commence. In July the Heads of Agreement for a ninety-nine-year lease for the air terminal was drawn up by IA (and then toned down by the SR) of which the more interesting clauses were:

No 9. The Southern Railway will, upon terms and conditions to be agreed, provide and operate on behalf of Imperial Airways and other transport companies using the Air Terminus, services of trains between the Air Terminus and the airports to be used by the services that lie within the area served by the Southern Railway.

The former 'Empire Terminal', now known simply as 157-197 Buckingham Palace Road, SW1, is Listed Grade II. The building has been restored in recent years for use by the National Audit Office, although they have been unable to alter the ballroom – now used for large meetings – due to its listed status. Apparently if the weather on the Solent was poor, Imperial Airways would deliberately retain their passengers and entertain them at Victoria rather than putting them on the train for Southampton. Unfortunately it is not a passenger train but instead a freight is passing. One cannot deny it is an impressive structure. *Hulton Getty*

In the case of the Empire services of Imperial Airways, the Southern Railway will operate special trains either steam or diesel-engined, or electric or other agreed type, with a view to giving the fastest possible, rapid and (most) comfortable accommodation between the Air Terminus and the airport.

No 10. The special trains are to be operated at the highest speed permitted by technical and operating conditions, and to timetables to be agreed and the Southern Railway will use its best endeavours to meet Imperial Airways reasonable requirements.

No 12. The special trains will be either owned by Imperial Airways and operated by the Southern Railway, or both owned and operated by the Southern Railway. In either event the charges to be made to Imperial Airways shall be calculated on 'most favoured nation' terms and the charge for each passenger shall not exceed the ordinary first class passenger fare for a similar distance.

So far so good, but the major issue still remained of a suitable airport site, which had yet to be confirmed. Eventually, in January 1935 Langstone Harbour (at the back of Portsmouth and usually referred to as Langston by the SR) was decided upon. On the surface it was also a sensible choice as here could be a combined landplane and flying boat base where shipping did not impinge. The scheme, which Portsmouth Corporation were to finance, envisaged a barrage across the harbour so that it created in effect a non-tidal lagoon. The whole, in general that is, seemed rather grand and in advance of its time. For its part, Portsmouth Corporation wanted a 75% guarantee from the Government but were dismayed in August 1936 to be told by the Air Ministry this would be no more than 40%.

Matters were dragging their heels for the EAMS, already the owners of twenty-seven flying boats and eight landplanes, and with the service intended to be progressively introduced early in 1937. Consequently, time was getting short to have some new facilities ready for the start.

Already IA had sensed that if reliance was placed on others to provide flying boat airport facilities the service would never get 'off the ground' consequently it was resolved to use Hythe on the western side of Southampton Water as the maintenance base and to ferry passengers to and from a temporary site at Southampton for boarding and alighting purposes: that is until permanent passenger facilities became available either at Langstone or wherever elsewhere. Because night flying facilities were not available at Hythe, it was essential to fly early in the mornings and therefore at an EAMS meeting on 18 February 1936 the departure time was set at 8.30am 'provided suitable sleeping coach facilities can be provided for transporting passengers from Waterloo to Southampton.' By the end of April IA had designated Southampton as the temporary base. (An interesting thought: with a maximum journey time by train between London and Southampton of likely ninety minutes, perhaps the idea was that passengers would board sleepers in London and remain in these vehicles overnight whilst parked in some isolated siding.)

Backtracking slightly, during the summer of 1936 J.L. Harrington of the SR (latterly Chief Officer administration for the SR) had become involved with IA regarding the siting of the new short branch to Langston Airport Terminal. This was separate from the existing Hayling Island branch and would instead leave the Havant-Farlington Junction section of the Portsmouth direct main line a few chains to the east of Farlington Junction and curve around southwards, across a new bridge and on to a new sea wall, to the terminus station. Not much more than half-a-mile long, it was estimated, complete with station and third rail for electric traction, to cost £93,250, which figure would go into the airport development costs rather than being borne by the SR. A station at the junction, to be provided by the Southern, was hinted at, but the railway did not encourage this notion. It is also interesting to note that there is no mention of any usefulness of the existing Hayling Island branch.

Some curious ideas seem to have emerged as to how long the journey from London Victoria to Langston Airport would take, for at a meeting at the Admiralty on 30 October 1936 the Air Ministry representatives are on record as stating, 'The Southern Railway had guaranteed a 55-minute service to Langstone, which was only ten minutes longer than the present time taken from London to Croydon' (that was of course, by road). Just how this misconception had arisen is not

By 1931, mail transported by air from Australia was reaching Britain in just sixteen days – less than half the time taken by sea. In that year, government tenders on both sides of the world invited applications to run new mail and passenger services between the ends of the British Empire. Australia's Qantas and Britain's Imperial Airways won with a joint bid. They then formed a joint company: Qantas Empire Airways, or QEA. QEA's new ten-day service between Rose Bay in Sydney Harbour and Southampton was so successful with letter writers that soon the quantity of mail was exceeding aircraft storage space. Then in 1934 the British Government decided to instigate an airmail service for the whole Commonwealth at fixed rates. For this purpose, Imperial Airways contracted Short Brothers to create a new form of flying boat, big and long range. These were known as the Short Empire and were called 'C' class because all had names starting with C, such as *Cooee*, *Cleopatra* and *Coogee*.

clear, possibly a simple typing error that was not picked up – likely for 55 read 85 – as a fifty-five-minute timing would have meant that these Langstone trains would have been the fastest in the Empire, even outstripping the LNER streamliners and over a Southern route infested with speed restrictions in the London area and a multitude of level crossings along the coast (assuming the Victoria-Sutton-Horsham-Barnham-Havant route was used). It is all the more interesting how the fifty-five-minute timing might have been considered possible as the third-rail electric multiple sets were restricted to a maximum speed of 75mph. Nonetheless, the misconception, if even in reduced form, persisted, for in a 1945 report there is a reference to a timing of one hour and thirty-five minutes, with a note of 'presumably less in peacetime'. A slower ninety-five-minute schedule to Langston would seem a far more realistic figure than even the perhaps omitted eighty-five.

Langstone Airport never materialised, of course. The barrage scheme was rejected in favour of a tidal scheme and there was a lot of acrimony as to whose fault it was that the proposal failed. Certainly Portsmouth Corporation did not like the look of a cost of £1,348,343 and threw it out by three votes. Around the same time proposals were made by the Air Ministry for a marine airport at Netley to be served by electric trains from Victoria via Havant and even, it has been suggested, another at Warsash with a 2.2-mile rail branch, complete with junctions facing each direction, from the Fareham-Southampton line. (Netley, of course, already had a branch to the military hospital there – see image in the previous issue of *SW*.)

None of these ideas was of much use to IA, still less yet another suggested base – this time at Lullingstone in Kent – as the flights were intended to start in earnest in January 1937. Consequently, temporary arrangements were made to use facilities at Southampton docks, the SR helping out with office accommodation and a room on the first floor of Canute Chambers (at the Docks) being placed at IA's disposal in December 1936, this with the approval of Sir Herbert Walker.

Flying boat *Caledonia* had already made some mail flights in December 1936 and although regular services were not scheduled to start until 6 February 1937 a number of flights prior to that were undertaken. It was one of these that triggered off the start of the railway supporting service: 'C' class flying boat *Centaurus* (identified as G-ADUT) unexpectedly arrived on 15 January from Alexandria with eight passengers, who were very speedily transferred from Hythe to Southampton Docks and into a Pullman coach, which was worked round to Southampton Central and there attached to the 5.20pm train – the Bournemouth Belle in fact – for Waterloo. The following day the first down service was operated, a Pullman and van attached to the 8.30am from Waterloo that, upon arrival at Southampton Central, were hauled to berth 50 in the docks whence launches took the passengers to join *Centaurus* at Hythe.

The quoted 'unexpected arrival' of *Centaurus* does, we admit, sound strange to say the least. Should we therefore take it exactly as written when it is said to have been 'unexpected', or was communication between the departure point and arriving location poor or even non-existent at this time? Eighty years later we can accept that messages were then limited to telegrams and possibly the telephone but surely there would be a lodged flight plan especially as passengers were on board? Might this even have been a deliberate act by IA/EAMS, who likely knew full well what was happening but who deliberately kept the railway 'in the dark' to test or even force them into action?

For the first regular flight on 6 February the same procedure was adopted as in January, unfortunately *Castor* (G-ADUW) developed mechanical trouble on becoming airborne and had to return with the result that it was not until two days later it was able to leave.

The Southern Railway provided a Pullman car – often *Lydia* complete with IMPERIAL AIRWAYS EMPIRE SERVICE roofboards, which was sufficient for the maximum of twenty-five passengers that a flying boat could accommodate, and a corridor guard's brake van as the special 'train'. Meals on the train were included in the air fare and an IA flight clerk travelled on the outward service to weigh passengers and baggage on a machine installed in the van for the purpose, for which reason a corridor connection luggage van was imperative – the idea of weighing passengers may sound quaint nowadays (what might any female passengers have thought is not mentioned) but is in fact little different to a modern day airline where a set weight is calculated for an 'average' passenger and seating arranged accordingly.

PULLMAN
THE EMBODIMENT OF MODERN TRANSPORT

Imperial Airways
Empire Flying-Boat
PULLMAN
Car Train,
Waterloo to
Southampton,
connecting with
EMPIRE
AIR MAIL
SERVICES

230
PULLMAN CARS
are now in
operation
on the
Southern,
L.N.E.R. and
Metropolitan
Railways.

PULLMAN CAR COMPANY, LIMITED.
Victoria Station, London, S.W.1.

Telegraphic Address: Telephone:
"Pullman, Rail, London."   Victoria 9978 (2 lines).

1938

It was customary to work this special to Southampton as a portion attached to the 8.30am down service and in the up direction coupled to a London-bound train. In the event that there was not a suitable up service available the portion became a train in its own right and worked straight up from the Docks to Waterloo.

Later, when the flying boat schedules were amended from late to early morning departures, the portion came down from London at the rear of the 7.30pm from Waterloo, was detached at Eastleigh and then worked as a special train to Southampton Terminus. The passengers were accommodated overnight in the adjoining South Western Hotel, IA having in the meantime found out that the SR did not possess any sleeping cars (which would have avoided such a transfer). It would indeed have been a nice touch to have had sleepers worked to the appropriate berth in the docks. Perhaps IA had simply assumed that every railway company possessed such vehicles, or maybe the question was never asked and the SR simply did not volunteer the information!

At first there were two departures a week by flying boat but this was built up month by month until the EAMS schedule in full, as originally envisaged, was reached in June. In September the launches transferred to Berth 9 in the Outer Dock, where there was rail access and handling facilities. For the winter of 1937–38 (October to April) the down service was provided by a special train leaving Waterloo (Platform 9) at 7.15am made up of one corridor third, one Pullman and a corridor third brake often with a 'King Arthur' engine as the power (Nos 738 and 780 were noted). From April there was a reversion to the old arrangements of detaching the two coaches from the 7.30pm from Waterloo at Eastleigh, where a 'King Arthur' class 4-6-0 locomotive (Nine Elms shed duty 54) would attach to take the train onwards. When there was a detachment from the 8.30am ex-Waterloo at Southampton Central, a T9 class 4-4-0 (Fratton shed duty 359) was booked to haul the coaches into the Docks. On the inward special trains T3 class 4-4-0 No 571 was reported on more than one occasion in August and September 1938 while another time No 461, a 4-6-0 of class T14, provided the power.

Historically, the Southampton Harbour Board had lobbied in December 1935 for the air base but were told in April 1936 that Langstone was the preferred location so there must have been some wry smiles when Imperial Airways decided in 1938 to change the status of Southampton from its temporary to the permanent base and set up stages in the New Docks. For a short period Berth 101 was used but then in August operations were moved to Berth 108, which allowed trains to use the Millbrook – Western Docks – exit. From 5 June the following year, the new London terminal building at Victoria was opened and this completely altered the railway operations. The outward route was now by way of Victoria to Clapham Junction, Balham, Streatham Junction and Tooting to Wimbledon, where the main Waterloo-Southampton route was gained. Inward the train left the main line at Wimbledon and travelled via East Putney to Clapham Junction and Longhedge Junction to get into platform 17 at Victoria.

The service operated daily except Mondays and Saturdays in the outward direction and daily, with two trains on Mondays, inwards. The booked times were Victoria depart 8.5pm arriving Southampton Terminus at 9.48pm – overnight hotel – and Southampton Docks depart 1.23pm with arrival at Victoria at 3pm. The extra Monday up service left the Docks at 12.37pm and was due in London at 2.14pm. Eastleigh shed had both duties allocated to it for working with T9 class 4-4-0 engines; the main duty was No 276, which was up with the 1.23pm and down with the 8.5pm, and the Monday up service was strangely allocated as duty 276A (instead of No 304, which was spare and could have been used in preference to the letter suffix). Eastleigh men worked the trains with a conductor from Stewarts Lane shed for the Victoria-Wimbledon and Clapham Junction-Victoria parts of the journey, for whom special stops had to be made. Considering that the engines had to be worked back on three occasions each week possibly without a booked load and that IA 'on time' allowance was six hours (comparable to present day BR practice of ten minutes), it sometimes meant that Stewarts Lane shed had to find an engine at short notice to power an equally quickly mustered set of carriages to form the outward train (because the inward service would be too late for the booked turn-round). Overall it would appear that the SR had not got too good a bargain for all their trouble.

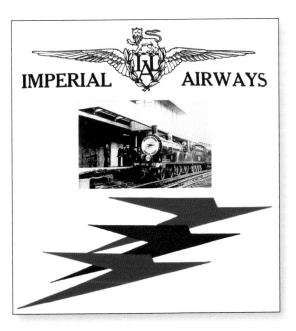

Be that as it may, the inaugural run from the new Victoria Terminal (by then named Airways House) and the adjacent platform 17 took place on 6 June 1939 with T9 class No 338, complete with circular headboard on the smokebox door with 'Speedbird' motif in the centre and IMPERIAL AIRWAYS SPECIAL TRAIN around the perimeter, with a three-coach train consisting of corridor brake composite, Pullman car and corridor guard's luggage van. Dinner was served en route on what was claimed as the first occasion on which air passengers had travelled by special train from a private railway station attached to an air terminal.

CARRIAGE WORKINGS.

The undermentioned workings supersede those advised by Special Notice 203 S.O.O., dated 30th June, 1939.

Three specially formed sets, each consisting of the following vehicles will be allocated to work the service between Victoria - Southampton and vice versa :-

Formation of special trains.

Leaving Victoria.	Leaving Southampton Docks.
1 C. Bke. Compo	1 C. bogie van
1 Pullman Car	1 Pullman Car
(Kitchen trailing)	(Kitchen leading)
1 C. bogie van	1 C. Bke. Compo

The Pullman cars will be roof boarded "Imperial Airways - Empire Service."

The cor.bke.compo and Guard's van will be equipped with small side destination boards "Imperial Airways".

A spare set of large and small boards will be held at Southampton Docks for emergency purposes.

In the event of any of the sets being diverted from the rostered workings the roof boards to be removed and placed in the Guard's van until required for airway services.

Southampton Docks to arrange for gas and water tanks to be replenished prior to each service.

Contemporary carriage working and formation notice.

When the special portions or trains had first started in 1937 it appears that the customary special traffic and carriage workings notices were used to convey information about workings. It might not have been unreasonable to expect that with daily services instigated arrangements would be dealt with in the normal working timetables, carriage notices and the like, as from June 1939. On the contrary, they were instead dealt with under Headquarters special notice No 170 (in the same way that Royal trains were handled) and thus the ordinary working timetables never had a reference to any of the workings. Thus even though the trains were regularly booked, they were still dealt with as 'permanent' special traffic.

So rapid was the response to the EAMS that the volume of mail continued to increase very quickly and so taxed the service to deal with it because of lack of aircraft mail capacity coupled with aircraft losses. (These losses are not specified.)

In order to be able to deal with this influx of mail, IA suspended all passenger bookings by EAMS on 9 August, although still carrying passengers prior to that date. (We are not told if EAMS mail was handled via the Southampton sorting office or was also trans-shipped via the special trains.) This then became the first threat to the Southampton service, the coup de grace delivered by the declaration of war a few weeks later. By then IA had already moved to Poole (and were operational from 1 September), the regular Southampton specials thus having a life of just under three months.

With the exception of L12 class 4-4-0 No 415 and 'Schools' No 919, the latter used once when returning from Eastleigh works after overhaul, all the journeys that can be traced have yielded T9 class 4-4-0s as having been used, the engine numbers as follows:

6 June	338	2 July	415	8 August	707
15 June	312	4 July	706	14 August	337
15 June	731	5 July	706	16 August	337
21 June	731	8 July	305	17 August	731
22 June	337	9 July	307	18 August	731
23 June	337	11 July	708	25 August	731
27 June	706	12 July	706	31 August	708
28 June	336	5 August	731		

Additionally, N class No 301 was employed by Stewarts Lane shed to cover for a late service and Nos T9s Nos 283, 303, 313, 314, 702, 724 and 725 were employed on other undated occasions. It would seem that the final pre-war train was that worked by No 708 on 31 August.

After the transfer to Poole there was a subsequent return but on a lesser scale to Southampton, and although this

With apologies for the quality, T9 No 338 at Victoria with the special working.

certainly did not involve the special trains there might have been a through coach or two as IA records indicate that the services were handled from Berth 1 and that train arrangements from there were readily organised. Subsequently, from 1 April 1940 Imperial Airways became British Overseas Airways Corporation and around the same time operations at Southampton again ceased once more in favour of Poole.

Backtracking slightly, from September 1939 the SR, along with the other main line railway companies, became part of the national Railway Executive and so had to make reference to that body for decision-making. Accordingly, a joint memo was sent from the SR and GWR to the Executive on 4 May 1942, stating that BOAC had requested train facilities for air passengers between London and Poole and also London and Bristol. For the Poole train Pullman cars would be used. Likely, there was more said behind the scenes as justification but it was duly approved for a commencement of the service on about 6 May 1942 with later reports that special trains were seen several times in June, so indicating the service had quickly become established even if subject to heavy delays in the up direction at times. (We may assume here that Mr Winkworth is referring specially to the SR service although he is not 100% clear on the matter.)

As an example of these delays – on the SR – on 5 July 1942, thirty-four passengers had disembarked from the flying boat at Poole at 11.30am and the SR had been requested to provide a train for departure at 1.15pm. The train was made ready in time but there was then a two-and-a-half hour delay before the passengers appeared at Poole station. The train eventually set off for Waterloo 154 minutes late yet still within the six-hour 'on-time' criteria of IA. No doubt this in turn caused delays both at Poole plus likely interruption to other workings on the up journey; the whole affair subject to a subsequent enquiry. This enquiry revealed that security checks, over which BOAC had no control, were the principal reason and that this had frequently occurred since May. The down train in the evening possibly ran to Bournemouth West so that passengers could avail themselves of hotel accommodation in the town.

The service was still operating in August 1943 but had been dropped by April 1944 when BOAC had to transfer their operations (temporarily as it transpired) from Poole to Neyland; not, as may be thought, due to an increasing threat of enemy action, but instead so that air and water space could be freed for the pending D-Day invasion. (The Neyland connection is briefly referred to in two books specific to the area. *Behind the Steam* and *Neyland – a Great Western Outpost*, both available from Kestrel Railway Books.)

Once the D-Day invasion had been mounted and was progressing satisfactorily, BOAC returned to Poole and the special trains recommenced from 15 September. Then, on 1 November, Hurn near Christchurch became an inland operational airport and to service operations there the special trains stopped at Christchurch, or reserved accommodation was made available on ordinary services. Hurn, of course, had been a station in its own right on the former Ringwood to Christchurch line but this had closed some years earlier. Finding

The cover of the *Southern Railway Magazine* for March 1937. Within was a two-page illustrated article – with images of the interior of the flying boats and no rail illustrations – written by E.J. Missenden, then the Traffic Manager of the SR – the whole centred primarily on the aviation part of the service.

accommodation though on the crowded trains of the period for passengers from Hurn joining at Christchurch was not easy, especially as the railway did not like making exceptions by reserving accommodation in a period when the general public were unable to do so. Hence once passengers/the party were seated, any unused reservations labels were removed so as not to further antagonise ordinary passengers.

In the spring of 1945 there were two identical train sets employed on the service with accommodation for 108 passengers in each, seventy-six of these being in first class. The formation was a corridor brake composite, two Pullman kitchen cars (*Flora*, *Medusa*, *Pearl*, *Philomel*, *Plate* and *Viking* were all noted) and a corridor brake first. The four vehicles gave a total train weight of 145 tons, although this was increased later in the year with the addition of a van – on one occasion Ferry Van No 2, formerly working as part of the Night Ferry service, was even noted.

The down special left platform 17 at Victoria at 7.00pm, calling only at Christchurch at 9.19pm before terminating at Bournemouth West at 9.39pm. It was thus one of the few passenger services ever to omit the Southampton stop. Road transport was then used to a hotel and subsequently for the final few miles to Poole. Bournemouth crews seem to have

Pullman car *Flora*, one of those used in the 1945 formation. It is seen here at the Pullman Works at Preston Park, Brighton. Notice the 'guard' wording on the end door. *Antony Ford*

dominated the work except on the occasions when the timings were altered to suit VIPs, or by the weather and other extraneous circumstances. In such circumstances a locomotive might also be supplied from Stewarts Lane. Stan Symes in his book of locoman's reminiscences, *55 Years on the Footplate: Reminiscences of the Southern at Bournemouth* (Oakwood Press, 1995), makes much mention of the working of both the up and down trains during the Second World War including one occasion when they had nothing more than a former SECR O1 0-6-0 for the down train from Victoria!

The up service, which now ran via Tooting instead of as previous via East Putney, due to revised track arrangements west of Wimbledon, had a two hour thirty-five minute timing – that is when it could get a road. Booked away at 3.24pm (later 3.00pm), it could and often did run late, indeed the records for February 1945 show that on one occasion departure was not until as late as 6.45pm. A random collection of arrival times at Victoria indicate the variations suffered:

21 January 1945	8.00pm
10 June 1945	9.05pm
13 July 1945	6.50pm
18 January 1946	6.40pm

Derek Winkworth comments that, 'Not unnaturally it was also not a popular turn for railwaymen in the up direction although when the number of passengers fell below 20 it did not operate, ordinary scheduled services to and from Waterloo being used instead.' (This is not borne out by similar comments from Stan Symes. Whatever the cause, if the down train did run but then the up was cancelled, this would, of course, then mean a set of stock was now located at the wrong end of the line. Likely it was worked back attached to another up direction working.)

Despite also having now entered the era of the Bulleid types, T9 4-4-0s were still very much to the fore, those noted including Nos 113, 118, 286, 305, 312, 713, 718, 719 and 828. Other locomotive types were also seen, including D1 Nos 1735, 1741, 1743, 1745 and 1749, E1 Nos 1160, 1165, 1179, 1497 and 1511, L class Nos 1760, 1761, 1763, 1764 and 1765, L12s Nos 415 and 420, as well as odd types including U No 1623, S11 No 399, V No 934 and even, it is said, a Q1, although no number is given. The Eastern Section classes were noted as appearing less frequently after mid-1945, which may be indicative of a change of roistering. At least two of the T9s, No 366 and one other, were fitted with speedometers in September 1945. One of these is illustrated in the Irwell Press volume on the class with the comment that the fitting was removed in the autumn of 1946. Crew rostering also changed with Bournemouth men working the up train and Stewarts

On board the 'Airways Special', Inspector Badger discusses travel arrangements with a lady passenger in car *Niobe*, in January 1946. After this date this car was transferred to service on the 'Golden Arrow'. To quote Antony Ford, 'According to Pullman Inspector Badger (as he then was), a familiar figure on the pre-war "Golden Arrow", the passengers on the Imperial Airways special trains during WW2 also included private soldiers and non-commissioned officers who were going on important secret duties overseas and were urgently required there, besides business men and others going abroad on urgent war missions. Indeed during the period 1942–45, more than 30,000 passengers used the service.' *Reference PULLMAN PROFILE No 5 by Antony Ford*

Lane in charge of the down run, using a pool of men who had previously been at Nine Elms and were therefore familiar with the Bournemouth line. This change of rostering might also go some way to explaining the appearance of SECR loco types.

With peace restored the justification to operate the trains as essential wartime services changed and commercial attitudes began to reassert themselves. As restrictions on travel were also lifted the SR anticipated a big upsurge in passenger traffic from the summer of 1946 onwards but with the continuing shortages of men and equipment it came as no real surprise when BOAC were advised that in order to maintain the service a minimum loading of 100 persons was required.

This was hardly borne out when compared with actual passenger numbers: for example in March 1946 there was an average loading of just forty passengers for the twenty down trains that operated, in the up direction the figures were slightly improved with twenty-eight trains and an average loading of fifty-one persons.

Pullman car *Ibis* sees duty on the Empire Service Imperial Airways working. The customs shed is likely at Southampton. *Antony Ford*

The situation was not helped when BOAC requested a morning departure from Victoria in the summer of 1946; but to this request the railway responded there were no paths available. Compromise suggestions by the SR that the 9.30am or 10.30am departures from Waterloo might be used were not well received by BOAC and they abruptly terminated the agreement stating that no further special trains would be required after 13 April 1946. A brace of T9s were used for the final working, No 286 down and No 728 up.

Although this was the end of the story so far as special trains was concerned, it was not the end of the BOAC/SR relationship. BOAC now commenced to ferry their passengers to and from London by road but no doubt due to the vehicles available and road network this was not at all popular. The whole was also not helped by refreshments of, according to Winkworth, 'doubtful quality' made available at the halfway stop. (We are

not told at this stage where this en route stop was made.) Aware of what was clearly a deterioration, regular passengers switched back to rail, even if to do so meant additional expense out of their own pockets. The BOAC manager at Poole despaired of the situation and more than once attempted to resort to a similar working as previously but to no avail. In the autumn of 1946 the coach service bordered on the ridiculous: 3.00pm departure from London, tea at Basingstoke (was this the location of the poor service ...?) and dinner at the Harbour Heights Hotel, Poole, at 7.30pm. Then it was as if a partial climb down was made, for BOAC announced that if there were fewer than six booked passengers the coach would not run and instead the travellers were to be issued with rail tickets.

Around the same time a further announcement was made that Poole was now to be phased out and a return made to Southampton Docks and Berth 50. Here a two-storey passenger handling building was constructed and the platform at nearby Berth 51 adapted with the provision of a covered way from the south end of the platform ramp connecting it to the new building. At this point BOAC again opened negotiations with the SR but the railway were adamant that the minimum passenger requirement of 100 persons still stood. BOAC then considered the use of helicopters from London to Southampton but it was quickly ruled out, cost most likely but possibly a lack of take-off/landing areas was another reason. With Southampton completed, Poole's last flying boat operation was on 30 March 1948 and Berth 50 at Southampton became operational the next day.

With the Docks at Southampton railway owned (it is convenient to ignore nationalisation on the point) it is not surprising that the railway hierarchy were still involved in what was the official opening of the Southampton facility on 14 April 1948. Sir John Elliot from the Southern Region and Lord Nathan, Minister of Civil Aviation, were some of the VIP party that arrived on special coaches attached to the 9 30am from Waterloo. These vehicles were detached at Southampton Central and worked around to Berth 50, arriving at 11.45am. Customary speeches were made, one of which was perhaps more in anticipation than fact, 'The building has been provided with its own special platform and siding so as to give the quickest and most comfortable connection between Southampton and London. Although special trains are not possible today I hope that the volume of traffic will justify this before too long.'

The two-coach special with its VIP compliment departed at 2.45pm, ironically also (and apart from an RCTS Special in 1953) the first and last time a passenger working of any type graced the platform at Berth 50.

Now as before, regular flying boat passengers avoided the road coaches, even if the London-Southampton road journey was shorter than that to Poole, and once again requested a rail ticket, so they could avail themselves of a meal en route, albeit at their own expense. Meanwhile, the files at BOAC bulged with complaints re the road travel: windows stuffed with newspaper to stop rattling, full ashtrays and other *minutiae*, none perhaps serious in itself but when combined this was not the service expected – nay, perhaps, even advertised.

Movement of flying boat passengers at Southampton appears to have peaked in May 1950 when 1,808 were handled, averaging sixty per day, still some way short of the guaranteed minimum required for the railway to consider the operation of a special train. The flying boat service too was also not even enjoying an Indian summer, the former Empire concept (it had now been renamed Commonwealth) also dying, and whereas in 1939 Imperial Airways was serving the Empire, in 1950 BOAC land-based aircraft were serving the world and it was thus in direct competition – with itself. The days of the flying boat were over and the last service operated to and from Southampton in November 1950.

There remained one ray of hope, which was the ongoing development of the Princess class of flying boat, a design able to carry 100 passengers, and with it a note on the BOAC file that perhaps with this a rail service might once again be possible. Sadly, the Princess class came to nought, only one ever flew (G-ALUN), and the hopes of a regular Southampton-New York service were dashed. All three built (or part built) were consigned to spend their days on land at Calshot until scrapped.

Rail-air co-operation, though, still exists though in today's market with Southampton Parkway station serving the adjacent airport, whilst a frequent and regular service operates from Victoria to Gatwick. In addition there are regular rail-air bus services from several stations; co-operation rather than confrontation being the now the order of the day.

I would like to thank Antony Ford for his permission to quote from his forthcoming *Pullman Profile No 5* with reference to the service and also draw the attention of the reader to an RMWeb thread that was opened on this subject in 2011 by Chris Leigh – probably stimulated by the Hornby release of their 'Flying Boat Train' pack; it may be found at:

www.rmweb.co.uk/community/index.php?/topic/33374-victoria-imperial-airways-terminal

Acknowledgement is also given to the original sources quoted by Mr Winkworth, namely British Airways for allowing the author (DWW) access to the Imperial Airways/BOAC files for research into the subject.

From the *Southern Region Magazine* of May 1968 (p.101), a BOAC flying boat is seen about to leave Berth 50 at Southampton. The new Marine Terminal is in the background.

Special train for the RCTS at Berth 50, 17 May 1953. Signs of (hoped for) past glory are present in the form of the public address loud speakers. Although of no relevance to the accompanying article, we may add that the tour of this date commenced at Eastleigh and ran first to Fawley, then to Southampton Docks and the Ocean Liner terminal, on then to Berth 50 and concluding at Southampton Central. Two locomotives were used, 30062 seen here and 30757 *Earl of Mount Edgcumbe*. *Arthur Taylor*

The Eastbourne Exhibition of 1951

No 7009 *Alfred the Great* passing Hampden Park 'ECS' en route to Eastbourne. The four, likely brand new, Mk1s had been collected from Battersea. *S.C. Nash/Stephenson Locomotive Society*

On Saturday, 2 June 1951 considerable local interest was aroused with an exhibition of British Railway's standard locomotives, freight and passenger rolling stock and signals in the goods yard at Eastbourne. The exhibition was arranged in connection with the conference of the International Union of Railways' being held in the town. Visiting the exhibits was restricted to the delegates for the morning, although the public were allowed access in the afternoon. (The UIC had been formed in 1922 with the aim of standardising industry practice certainly amongst adjoining countries whose rail networks might conjoin, but also elsewhere.

Until the advent of the Channel Tunnel, Britain's railways had, of course, remained mainly isolated, save limited cross-border co-operation with train ferry services. Since that time standardisation has become more widespread and nowadays there are numerous examples of former British locomotives working either temporarily or permanently away from home shores. One example of early co-operation was in 1964 when the former Western Region gas turbine engine No 18000 was handed over to the UIC for tests in connection with adhesion on lightweight bogies. Years later, its role over, No 18000 was subsequently returned to the UK and now resides with the Great Western Society at Didcot.)

For whatever reason, there appears to have been scant coverage of the Eastbourne event in the railway press, possibly because of the limited time available for public viewing. Fortunately it was covered in both the local newspapers, the *Eastbourne Gazette* and the *Eastbourne Herald*, and more particularly the *Railway Observer*, which carried some notes both of the displays and the workings of the exhibits to and from Eastbourne. These notes and the captions to this article draw heavily on the *R.O*, whilst the images are from the archives of the Stephenson Locomotive Society (with grateful thanks to Gerry Nichols) and also the collection of the late Arthur Taylor.

A total of six locomotives and other items were exhibited in the station goods yard, intended to represent the latest and best in modern traction – unless there was a theme of which we are not aware? Setting aside the last comment, why these six and not others is not explained, especially as there could well have been others that might equally have claimed a part: main line diesels Nos 10000/1, 10201/2, a representative of the electric EM1 class, EMUs etc, etc. (There is justifiable reason why gas turbine 18000 might not have been present as it would likely have been foul of gauge.) It certainly cannot have been for reason of distance either; witness the 'Fell' diesel being present. Perhaps it was a simple case of logistics for the limited time the exhibits would be on show. Whilst we also glean an amount from the illustrations themselves, no definite information has been found referring to the rolling stock and signalling displays. Was there even a brochure produced? In which case, has anyone a copy?

At this stage it is appropriate to list the locomotives that were present, diesels 10100 and 15227 (the latter 73C, Hither Green), electric locomotive 20003, and steam engines, 70009 (70A, Nine Elms), 73001 (17A), and 75000 (82C), thus it can be seen that certainly not all the stock was Southern Region based.

Access was restricted to the delegates, of which there had been in excess of 200 at the conference, on the Saturday morning; but the event was then thrown open to the public in the afternoon. The three steam engines were literally brand new, all three having been released to traffic the previous

month. – the BR delegates included Messrs R.G. Jarvis, J. Elliott, and R. Bourn, the last named the assistant Continental Superintendent of the Southern Region.

To reach the event, No 73001 worked south light engine via Brent, Barnes and Battersea Yard. No 75000 towed diesel 10100, although where this was collected from is not stated; possibly from Battersea, for reasons that will be seen later. Probably for weight constraints over bridges, a bogie vehicle was placed between the two engines, with the diesel thought to have been hauled dead. The 'Britannia' took four coaches as part of the display, also from Battersea. Certainly the last two mentioned journeys occurred on Friday, 1 June so it may be reasonable to suppose all three were on the same day.

Electric 20003 worked down light from Selhurst on the evening of 1 June but developed a hot box and was forced to travel to Brighton for attention after the exhibition. No details are given as to the movement of the shunter 15227, although we know it was a Hither Green-based machine.

Upon arrival at Eastbourne, E4 No 32485 was used to shunt the exhibits into position and this implies the fires were thrown out of the steam engines. This seems to be confirmed as there is no sign of steam or smoke from the engines whilst on display.

Arrived at Eastbourne. Already attached to the rear is 'E4' 32485 ready to remove the coaching stock from No 70009. One lady visitor, when visiting the Mk1 kitchen car later, described the modern kitchen as 'a housewife's dream'. *S.C. Nash/Stephenson Locomotive Society*

A pristine No 20003, at the time three years old but having had a recent repaint at least – perhaps for display? It is seen being shunted also by No 32485. In the background the station canopy is evidence of the bombing of the railway in the Second World War. *Arthur Taylor*

Having been turned, No 70009, with 73001 alongside, await to be formed into procession and then shunted into position. As with the previous view, the engine shed too shows how it was blitzed in the war. *Arthur Taylor*

The three steam engines being manoeuvred into position. *Arthur Taylor*

Pristine and ready for inspection. This would have been the first visit of any of the BR Standard types to Eastbourne, although the 73xxx would become regular visitors in later years. Behind we have the first view of the 'Fell' diesel, certainly the one and only time it ever ventured on to Southern Region metals.
S.C. Nash/Stephenson Locomotive Society

Lined up and ready for viewing. We cannot know if the items of rolling stock on the right were also part of the display, although the local newspaper did mention 'goods trucks'. *Arthur Taylor*

A popular event with footplate access possible. The local newspaper the *Eastbourne Gazette* commented in its edition of 6 June that more than 3,000 people had attended. It must be recalled that austerity was only just starting to release its grip at this time; indeed some household foods were still rationed. Consequently, any form of entertainment or show was welcome. *S.C. Nash/Stephenson Locomotive Society*

The 'Fell' 4-8-4 (later converted to a 4-4-4-4). This is likely taken just before or just after the show as there are no visitors present. We know that during the show, or certainly for part of it, some of the bodyside access panels were opened to allow a view of the 'innards'. Whether or not footplate access was possible is not recorded. The designer Colonel Fell was present and as was reported in the contemporary press '… assisted his 89-year-old mother on to the footplate'. Notwithstanding, one cannot say it was a particularly attractive machine. The track in the foreground without ballast may have been part of the p/way exhibit. *Arthur Taylor*

The intention had been for the electric locomotive, 20003, to later haul the delegates' train, consisting of twelve LMR coaches for a trip to Bath but in the event No 20001 was called upon and arrived light taking the train as far as Reading, via Streatham Common, Streatham, Haydons Road, Wimbledon, Weybridge and Ascot. It returned the same evening via Westbury.

The various exhibits were dispersed on Sunday, 3 June so lighting up would have occurred either late on Saturday or early Sunday morning.

For the return, No 75000 towed the 'Fell' diesel to Battersea and then proceeded on to Swindon. No 10100 was observed standing alone outside Stewarts Lane shed both before and after the event, until the arrival of No 73001, which

No 20001, which arrived as a hurried replacement for the failed 20003. This took the delegates' train to Reading, where a steam engine took its place. *Arthur Taylor*

No 70009 lit up and ready to return on Sunday, 3 June. Other engines visible include No 31812, possibly 32583, and another member of the E5 class and a K. On the footplate of No 70009 is a Loco Inspector complete with his 'bowler hat' badge of office – an inspector had been present on the footplate of No 70009 during at least the afternoon and would explain the controls to the visitors. According to the S.C. Nash records, the photograph was definitely taken on 3 June, which would imply No 70009 had been tuned again to face the shed following the display… *S.C. Nash/Stephenson Locomotive Society*

took over returning the diesel to the LMR, presumably to Derby. We are not told what comments were made about it upon its temporary sojourn there! Nos 15227 and 70009 returned, we think light engine, to their respective SR depots and the passenger rolling stock at least was returned to Battersea behind No 31816.

and is now seen reversing away ready to return to Nine Elms. *S.C. Nash/Stephenson Locomotive Society*

As with many newspaper reports of an event there was likely some judicious journalistic licence in a piece that appeared in the *Herald*, although it is included much of interest under the heading 'Mad about Engines':

Hundreds of people who flocked to the exhibition, held in connection with the International Union of Railways conference, at Eastbourne station goods yard on Saturday, were too busy admiring the giant locomotives to notice an old lady being wheeled through the crowds in a bath chair. She was entranced by the big driving wheels, and the maze of pistons and pipes towering above her, but her old bath chair with polished acetylene lamps, looked a little out of place beside these modern 'titans of the track'. I could not help wondering if she was indeed a railway enthusiast, or whether her 'chauffeur', cherished an interest in trains from his school days, and it was he who had dragged her there willy-nilly. I asked her why she had preferred to take her Saturday afternoon airing at Eastbourne goods yard, rather than along the promenade. 'Well, you see,' she said, 'I am mad about engines. All my life I have wanted to be an engine driver, and when I was young I used to stand for hours on station platforms watching locomotives shunting up and down the track.'

'Alas, not for me,' she paused then added, a trifle wistfully: 'I would give anything to go for a ride in one of them, even at my age, but unfortunately, I cannot walk very far, and I should never be able to climb up in to the driver's cab.' Although she has always had a passion for railway engines, she admitted that she was not mechanically-minded. I should never learn how to drive one, what with all the dials and levers. But I should let others do the driving so that I could sit back and enjoy the thrill of speeding along. 'Instead of that I have to be content with being wheeled around in a bath chair.' A little later I turned around just in time to see her old chair being swallowed up by the crowd as it jogged along towards the exit. I am sure she obtained as much enjoyment from her visit as any of the youngsters who left the exhibition with hands covered in axle grease and faces begrimed with coal dust.'

Some further images of the movement of stock may also be seen on the J.J. Smith pages of the Bluebell Museum Photographic Archive.

Any further images and information on the 'Fell' diesel concerning its building, mechanics, operation, and demise would be most welcome.

With the 'Fell' in tow again, No 75000 is en route to Stewarts Lane after the event. On this occasion the location is not reported.
S.C. Nash/Stephenson Locomotive Society

Caterham
Catering for the Commuter

Jeffery Grayer

Jeffery Grayer recalls the early days of the Caterham branch and its role serving the Surrey commuter for more than 160 years

A somewhat blemished, but nonetheless fascinating, view of the original Caterham station building taken sometime in the 1860s. Note the gentleman standing in the doorway sporting a top hat and the mineral wagon in the yard bearing the legend 'Clay Cross'. The very ornate station building is adorned with decorative barge boarding and period advertisements. The steep-sided nature of the attractive Caterham valley is apparent in this view, the unspoilt nature of which was largely eroded over the years with sprawling residential development. *RCHS/Spence collection*

In the mid-nineteenth century the small village of Caterham, yet to become the dormitory town of today, found itself in 'railway border country' and at the heart of the long-running dispute between the two mainline railway companies that operated in the area, namely the LBSCR and the SER. This feud, which has been well documented in railway literature, saw perhaps its biggest skirmish in the case of the Caterham Railway. This company was incorporated in June 1854 to construct a branch from Godstone Road, later to become Caterham Junction and then finally Purley in 1888, on the joint SER/LBSCR London-Redhill line, to Caterham. The terminus,

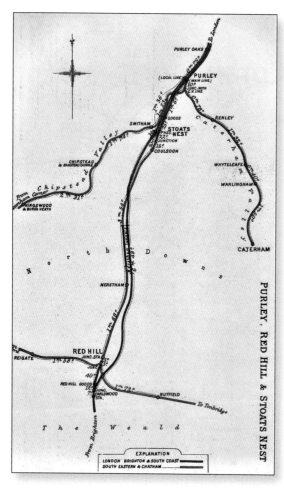

Railway Clearing House diagram of the LBSCR and SER lines in the vicinity of Caterham.

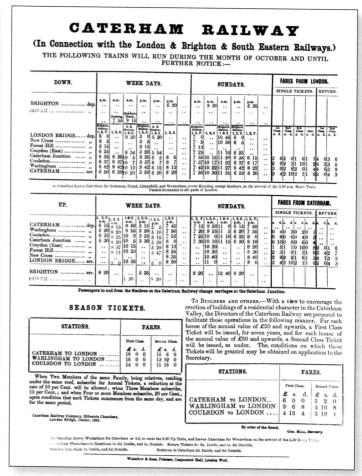

Timetable from 1856.

A venerable 2-4-0 locomotive graces this partially retouched view of Caterham station, which also shows to the left rear the engine shed that was later to become the goods shed. Amongst the 2-4-0 types operative on the branch were those of the SER's locomotive superintendent James Cudworth. *RCHS/Spence collection*

situated at the end of a 4¾-mile single-tracked branch line from the main London-Brighton line, was destined not to open its doors until August 1856, even though the line had been ready since the previous September. Delays were due to the intransigence of both the LBSCR and the SER in permitting the other to work the line. Indeed it was not until the Caterham Railway Co. obtained the use of a locomotive and carriages from the LBSCR that services could finally be inaugurated. Problems were apparent from the outset for whilst Caterham was judged to be in the SER's operational sphere, being east of the main Brighton line, the company's trains had no right to call at the junction station, which had in any event been closed since 1847 apparently for 'reasons of public safety' – an excuse not unfamiliar to modern ears. The junction station was finally reopened in November 1856 as Caterham Junction but the delaying tactics of the LBSCR led to it being sued by the Caterham company in the Court of Common Pleas.

The Caterham company ran at a loss right from the start, as much of the local agricultural population remained employed in the local area and had little spare funds to enjoy train travel. Commuting to the capital as we know it was in its infancy and hopes of significant freight traffic from local quarries failed to materialise in view of their distance from the railhead. The background of bickering between the LBSCR and the SER can hardly have helped the fledgling company to succeed: it was even unable to pay the full hire charges for carriages supplied by the LBSCR. The branch was eventually purchased for less than half its £30,000 cost of construction by the South Eastern Railway when the Caterham Railway went bankrupt in July 1859. Even when the SER had completed the purchase, continuing disagreements between the two mainline companies saw the LBSCR ban passengers who had travelled from SER stations from using their East Croydon station, insisting that all Caterham passengers travelling to East Croydon

The original station at Caterham seen shortly before its demolition in 1899. It lay at the foot of a steeply inclined carriage drive from the main road and presents a busy scene with a traction engine on the far right, the yard crane handling goods, and with parcels and passengers on the platform. Note both the old and new signal boxes, the latter seen in a later colour image in this feature, and two sets of starting signals in the left background. The spread of housing on the right is very noticeable in comparison with the scattered residences apparent in the earlier view. *RCHS/Spence collection*

The railway staff of Caterham pose in front of the original building with an SER luggage trolley. The staff shown number sixteen, a large but not unusual number in the Victorian age for what was essentially a rural branch terminus. *RCHS/Spence collection*

should hold LBSCR tickets. This was all but impossible as trains were timed to leave Caterham Junction before passengers could possibly have had a chance to rebook. Attempts were also made to prevent passengers entering SER mainline trains at the junction. A deluge of letters to *The Times* and a welter of critical articles finally forced the companies to see sense.

The line then settled down to a relatively uneventful existence. In response to the gradual spread of housing developments all down the valley it was decided to double the railway in 1897–99 and Caterham station was rebuilt in 1900. Electrification came to

the line in March 1928 in the initial part of the Central Section DC electrification programme covering the lines from London Bridge via Forest Hill to Caterham and Tattenham Corner, together with the spur from Sydenham to Crystal Palace Low Level. This scheme was to see the end of the original overhead AC electric system, which had opened in 1909 but did not venture as far as Caterham. Three coach electric sets were introduced to the Caterham line and these generally combined/split with services from/to Tattenham Corner at Purley. On race days separate self-contained race services were provided.

The timber platform is seen at Caterham Junction, subsequently renamed Purley in 1888, with the Caterham branch train waiting for the connection from the mainline in about 1880. The tall signal box was a feature of the junction station. The station was rebuilt by the LBSCR in 1889–90, providing six platforms; two for local services, two for expresses bypassing Redhill via the new Quarry line and two for SECR branch line services to Caterham and Tattenham Corner.
RCHS/Spence collection

Unloading rails and sleepers during the doubling of the branch, which was completed in 1899. *RCHS/Spence collection*

No 248 was one of the famous Cudworth Class 118 design and here the locomotive crew and the station staff at Caterham pose for the photographer in 1885. At one point this class formed half of the SER locomotive stock and it was easily the most numerous of Cudworth's designs. Although they were 2-4-0 tender locomotives, they were reputed to have spent as much as half their life working tender first. The initial member of the 127-strong class left Ashford Works in 1859 but No 248 seen above was built by Dubs & Co. in 1874 and was withdrawn in 1896. Incidentally, the hamper upside down on the platform (which someone will have to answer for) rather surprisingly appears to read 'Cowdung' – not the best receptacle for such a commodity one would have thought! *RCHS/Spence collection*

One of the intermediate stations on the branch is Kenley seen here after electrification. It is better known to railway aficionados as the location of one of the Battle of Britain airfields commemorated in the name of Bulleid Pacific No 34068. Service personnel tended to use the more conveniently located Whyteleafe station rather than Kenley, whose RAF airfield was operational in 1917–88. A similar style of 'Alpine' architecture to that provided at Caterham is apparent here. Prior to doubling of the line, a passing loop was provided and the station was known as Coulsdon until December 1856, when it was changed to Kenley to reflect the name of a nearby country seat. The chimney of the East Surrey waterworks is visible on the far right. *RCHS/Spence collection*

There were a few accidents on the branch, perhaps the most serious occurring at Caterham on 26 June 1945 when an up electric service left Platform 1 for Charing Cross against the signals and collided with an incoming service from London Bridge entering No 1 platform via a crossover under clear signals, resulting in the death of both motormen.

The centenary of the branch in 1956 was marked by the running of special 'Caterham Centenarian' trains using Stroudley 'Terrier' No 377s, the Brighton Works shunter, with red-liveried SECR birdcage carriage set No 580. Subsequently track rationalisation with the cessation of goods services in September 1964 saw much land sold off at the terminus.

Opposite top: **Another image full of period detail taken sometime in the early 1920s. Note the platform gas lamp, the white circles on the signal arms, later to be replaced by white bars, the second-class carriage compartments (there would be only first and third class after 1923) and the Caterham Electric Supply Co. with its tall chimney. This facility was formerly supplied with rail-borne coal.** *RCHS/Spence collection*

Bottom: **The three-coach set of the 3.18pm departure from Purley, hauled by Wainwright H Class 0-4-4 tank No A164, passes Purley East (former SER) signal box en route to Caterham on 22 May 1926. In the background are the overhead catenaries used by electric trains to Coulsdon North from 1 April 1925 until 22 September 1929. East signal box was to close in 1928 when Purley South box assumed its functions. A new signal box came into operation in 1955 superseding both Purley South and Purley North boxes.** *RCHS/Spence collection*

A quintessential timeless Southern Electric scene is captured in colour at Caterham during the 1960s. The green enamel running in board, the totem on the concrete lamppost with its typical SR octagonal shade, plus, of course, the semaphore signals on their bracket together with the adjacent signal box and 10mph speed restriction signs, all add to the period charm of the view. Human interest is added by the figure of the signalman seen outside his box with watering can in hand attending to the display of colourful blooms and climbers rambling up the signal box steps. It is quite probably his motorised velocipede parked at the platform's end. The platform and some rationalised track remain today but all the remaining infrastructure seen here has vanished in the name of progress.

Caterham signal box closed in September 1983 when it came under the control of Purley, which in turn closed in January 1984 when Three Bridges Signalling Centre took control of signalling on the Brighton line south of Anerley and Thornton Heath, including both the Caterham and Tattenham Corner branches. A plaque was unveiled at Caterham station in 2006 marking the 150th anniversary of the opening of the line.

Today the station and all trains serving it are operated by the Southern Train Operating Company, the branch having a line speed of 60mph. Caterham continues to have a single island platform with a one-storey ticket office and there is a carriage siding on the up side of the station catering for off-peak stock storage. It currently enjoys an off-peak service of four trains per hour to East

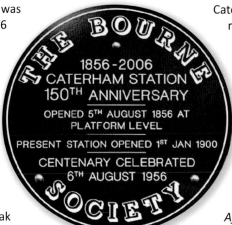

THE BOURNE

1856-2006
CATERHAM STATION
150TH ANNIVERSARY

OPENED 5TH AUGUST 1856 AT
PLATFORM LEVEL

PRESENT STATION OPENED 1ST JAN 1900

CENTENARY CELEBRATED
6TH AUGUST 1956

SOCIETY

Croydon, two of which continue to London Bridge whilst two proceed to Victoria. In 2015–16 Caterham station was used by some 1.128 million passengers, the majority of whom are regular commuters to the capital and to Croydon, a far cry indeed from those early days when the fledgling Caterham company struggled to make ends meet. Corresponding population growth has been rapid, rising from fewer than 200 in the early 1800s to 815 in 1856, 3,500 in 1871, reaching 12,000 in 1921 and 21,000 in 2011. The dramatic rise after the opening of the railway in 1856 is apparent from these figures.

For a full history of the Caterham Railway, the reader is referred to the Oakwood Press volume, *Caterham Railway: the Story of a Feud – and its Aftermath* by Jeoffry Spence.

Seeing Life in Colour
Some images from the lens of Tony Molyneaux

A brief trip down memory lane now with a colour feature from the lens of Tony Molyneaux. I have had the privilege of knowing Tony for several decades, a quiet man always willing to assist and with an interest in all forms of transport. His photographic excursions commenced in the mid-1950s and he was often accompanied by friends Les Elsey and occasionally Peter Gray. Indeed, Tony and Les might often be found standing side by side taking similar shots, and it is Tony who admits that he learnt a great deal about the ability to take good photographs from Les. Tony's collection runs to several thousand, but as mentioned above, this does include other forms of transport as well. An amount of his colour material has also appeared in various colour albums co-authored by Tony and myself and produced over the years by Ian Allan. We are delighted now to present a small selection of some that had been hidden away, one for more than sixty years.

The oldest in this batch of views is of 'Schools' No 30910 *Merchant Taylors* at Newhaven on 13 April 1958. This was the day of the fames RCTS 'Sussex Coast Limited' tour, which included the final run of the one remaining 'Brighton Atlantic', No 32424. We are not informed what duty the 'Schools' was being prepared for but it will be noted it is displaying an 'SPL' headcode disc.

Allbrook just north of Eastleigh and the entry point to the east yard. 'Class 5' No 73082 is in charge of a most interesting special working, reported by Tony as 'Electric stock from the Works'. Although we have a date, 19 June 1961, the weekly Special Traffic Notice for the period gives no information and so likely this was arranged, literally with a day or two's notice. Tony gives the information of 'Electric set No 6161 in tow', but this is certainly not the formation of any electric set I know – so best to ask an expert – enter Colin Marsden! 'What an interesting image. Well, 6161 is a 1957-design 2-HAP built for the Kent Coast. But what you have here might include one vehicle from the HAP, but is rather odd. The leading coach is a HAP vehicle, but the second and third are 4-EPB TS coaches. The fourth, fifth and sixth vehicles are SR EMUs, the two outer ones have roundels so they are motor cars. To me this is some test formation. In mid-1961 some trials were undertaken with various EMU coaches in an attempt to form up some trailer control (TC) sets but from paperwork these used non-powered DTS driving cars. The other interesting thing is that the steam loco is vacuum-braked and the EMU cars are air-braked, which cannot work together, so the train is being worked unfitted, hence the BV on the rear.'

Opposite top: 'U' No 31831 shunting the carriage sidings at Ilfracombe in mid-summer 1962 – 4 August to be exact. The intensity of the passenger workings to this Southern outpost may be gauged by the sheer number of vehicles in the yard, including a restaurant car. The vehicles that No 31831 is adjacent to are non-corridor and could well have come from a WR service via Taunton. Nowadays of course, people come by car or coach to this north Devon resort famous for its surf.

Bottom: Pull-push working; well, rather more pull than push at this point. The 12.08 Brockenhurst to Ringwood train ('old-road', of course) near Lymington Junction, the point where the train will turn off the main line. The date is 14 October 1961, No 30108 is already 57½ years old and will survive another three years being one of the final members of the class to cease work in May 1964, coinciding with the closure of the Ringwood line to passengers.

Another one a few yards north of the earlier view, this time No 34009 *Lyme Regis* on what is clearly a special working. Unfortunately Tony's records do not include a date this time, although from the serial numbers of other images taken around this time it is likely around September 1963. The headcode is for a special working between Southampton and Waterloo – other than a boat train – and is especially interesting considering the mixed livery stock. Tony was likely tipped off on this one, but any further information would be welcome.

Inter-regional working at Eastleigh, the evening of 28 May 1964. This is a through train between York and Bournemouth with 'Black 5' No 45493, at that time of Holyhead shed, in charge! (The engine later moved to Bescot and then Banbury, which would have made its appearance on such trains more likely.) Without having access to the locomotive workings for the day, there are any one of a number of reasons why this engine might have been used. In the 1960s various LM types were taken to Eastleigh for repair and then perhaps 'borrowed' to cover a shortage on the SR. It could also be that what was often a WR working south of Oxford was cancelled and the 'Class 5' substituted here. Whatever, it appears to have made an impression on the spotter standing on Platform 3!

Fresh from overhaul, 'Standard 5' No 73049 reposes in the sunshine in Eastleigh Works yard, 14 September 1963. *Railway Observer* records for the period indicate No 73049 together with sister No 73029 (then allocated to Weymouth) had arrived for works attention sometime between 10 June and 6 July. At the time this was a Bath Green Park engine, but she would move to Oxford towards the end of 1964. She was placed in store soon after and then withdrawn in spring 1965.

Another of Tony's early images, this is No 34055 *Fighter Pilot* seen at Southampton Central on 3 March 1957. The engine appears to be reversing down towards the station but we are not informed as to the subsequent working.

Six years on from the previous view, 'sometime in 1963', 'U' No 31804 was photographed from alongside the two sidings leading to and from Eastleigh steam shed as it passes with a down van train. The slope carrying the roadway up to Campbell Road bridge is visible on the left, whilst passing on the up line is either a passenger or ECS working.

'King Arthur' No 30763 *Sir Bors de Ganis* heads north into Popham Tunnel No 2 (198 yards). According to Tony, the view was recorded on 12 August 1961. No details are given as to the working but it could be an inter-regional service. Potentially there must be some doubt as the accuracy of the year stated as records indicate the engine was withdrawn in the autumn of the previous year. Whatever, the service has just left the 80ch curve through the station and is passing the end of the former Quarry sidings on the right, later used as a store in the Second World War and finally as a repository for stored/withdrawn rolling stock. Oh, if only the camera was just a little more to the right!

Almost the end of steam and a view impossible to recreate today as the M27 crosses over the railway at this point. In the spring of 1967, 24 April to be precise, a thoroughly grimy 'Class 4' No 76064 heads north towards Eastleigh with a mixed van train from Southampton containing examples of BR, SR, GWR, and LNER stock. No 76064 was allocated to the Southern Region from the start and remained an Eastleigh-based engine throughout its eleven-year life ending in July 1967.

Concluding (for the present) this colour feature, here is DS235, the former 30066 introduced into Southern Railway stock in May 1947 and reassigned into the departmental list in May 1963. It is seen at Eastleigh on 6 June 1963, probably soon after renumbering and will be noted as lettered for 'Lancing Works'.

The Strange Saga of No 41295

Nigel Tilly

On 14 November 1964 I set out from Canterbury West with Terry Phillips, a friend from school, to travel over the New Romney branch. My diary for the day records that outside Ashford Works I saw two of the last three members of C class locos and two 'USA' tanks, which, as the Ashford Works shunters, had been the last survivors of steam in East Kent for some. It also records the sighting of 'Ivatt Class 2' 2-6-2T No 41295, which was most certainly not expected, and the presence of which has remained unexplained to me for more than fifty years.

Normal steam working in East Kent had ended during 1962, and only the last three survivors of the once numerous C Class 0-6-0s remained to be used for snowplough duties in January 1963 before being confined to Ashford Works as yard shunters. Apart from the two 'USA' tank engines that joined them on these duties, the only other steam locos that I believe were ever seen east of Tonbridge during 1963–64 were two further 'USAs' loaned to Betteshanger Colliery.

Over the years that have elapsed since that sighting of No 41295 in Ashford I have often wondered what it was doing there, and have been especially glad that Terry was with me on the day in question since otherwise I might by now be thinking that I had been dreaming. I had decided in my own mind that the intruder was probably either covering for a short-term shortage of available works shunters, or being trialled as a possible alternative to the 'USAs', and left it at that.

However, a chance conversation at a recent 'Gauge 0 Guild' show with Geoff Roberts, who was also living in Canterbury when steam operations drew to a close, has recently opened up a new possibility. A former Ashford Works employee has claimed that No 41295 actually visited the works for a boiler change, this being well over two years after steam overhauls in the works had come to an end! The story goes that the boiler on No 41295 was condemned, but the loco was in otherwise good condition. Authority was given for an unscheduled boiler change, but Eastleigh had no capacity to undertake the work. Brighton had closed by then and so by fair means or foul, Ashford were asked if they were able to carry out a boiler change and they apparently responded, 'Yes, if a boiler is available': consequently the engine and a spare boiler duly arrived and the change was carried out.

At face value the story is not easy to believe, but the allocation history of No 41295 at this time is interesting and also relevant. I believe it was on the books at Wadebridge from February 1963 to June or July 1964, during which time Wadebridge moved from being a Southern depot to a Western one. In June 1964 it moved to Yeovil (still Western Region) then in September 1964 it returned to the Southern at Nine Elms, before moving on to Bournemouth in November 1964, where it stayed until near the end of Southern steam in 1967.

The inter-Regional move back to Nine Elms in September 1964 would no doubt have required some inspection by a Southern boiler inspector. It is therefore perfectly feasible from a timing point of view that this inspection led to the boiler being condemned, the boiler change at Ashford, and then the reallocation of the loco to Bournemouth when it left Ashford two months later in November 1964, due to developing operational needs.

Where then might the replacement boiler have been found? In autumn 1964 Eastleigh had just finished General Repairs on steam and so it is very possible that just at this time an overhauled boiler was in the works, ready for the next planned overhaul that never in fact took place. However, one can imagine that there might have been serious industrial relations problems if management were to be seen to export work to another location when numbers employed on steam overhauls were being reduced. This is not to say that a boiler could not have been supplied by Eastleigh but instead to highlight that it would not have been easily done. Indeed, moving one off site would likely also have been difficult to hide. There is an alternative hypothesis. Somewhere along the line there has been a story that 41260 was also at Ashford around this time, and the allocation history of this loco might just encourage this scenario because it was condemned at Bournemouth in September 1964. This leads to the possibility that it was condemned for mechanical reasons but with a good boiler. Ashford then received both Nos 41260 and 41295 and made one good loco out of the two: and No 41295 went off to Bournemouth as a direct replacement for No 41260.

The record cards of the two locos in question (if they still exist) may, or may not, substantiate some of the above. Even so, it does make a good story but can anyone provide hard facts to explain that sighting fifty-four years ago?

(We have searched high and low through the records we have at our disposal to find a specific image of either engine around this period but so far without success. Apologies to Nigel on this one, but I did say we would try. Can anyone help with an image, or add more to this fascinating saga? – Ed.)

Accident at Reading, 12 September 1855
A Dickensian Tragedy on the South Eastern Railway

John Burgess

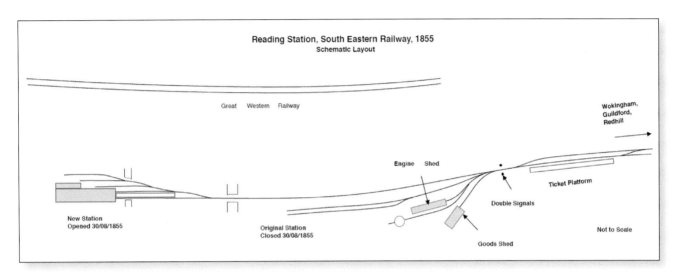

Reading Station, South Eastern Railway, 1855
Schematic Layout

Setting the scene

The Reading, Guildford and Reigate Railway opened its line from Redhill to Reading throughout on 20 August 1849, and from the outset the line was worked by the South Eastern Railway. Three years later, the SER absorbed the RG&R.

The first passenger terminus at Reading was located some way short of the forecourt to the Great Western Railway station. This temporary station on North Forbury Road later became part of the SER goods yard at Reading. The second station, located more conveniently close to the GWR station, was opened on 30 August 1855, just two weeks before the accident. It was connected to the original line by a single-track section of line about 600 yards long with a junction just beyond the throat of the temporary station. The new station consisted of a single island platform with two faces, with about half the station within a covered train shed. Also served from the junction was the original locomotive shed (located on the south side of the running line, and soon to be replaced by the three-road shed to the north of the running line, which lasted until the end of steam in the 1960s), and next to it the goods shed. At the junction was a pair of double signals ostensibly covering movements in and out of the station, the yard and the goods and engine sheds – see the schematic plan showing the location of all these elements, which is based on a plan appended to the 1855 Accident Report.

The Board of Trade was charged with the investigation of railway accidents, and from the 1840s a succession of Railway Inspectors carried out these duties. They were selected from amongst the senior officers of the Royal Engineers and at the time of the Reading accident, Captain H.W. Tyler was officiating. Accidents were subject to formal inquiries reported to Parliament but it is fair to say that the powers of the Inspectorate were limited

Early photographs of the South Eastern at Reading are conspicuous by their absence, indeed photographs of the Southern in the area are similarly dwarfed compared with those of that 'other railway'. We have little choice then but to introduce this piece with a view that has been seen before elsewhere but is as early as we can get showing the SER station having just two platforms and an overall roof. Its larger and better known neighbour is to the right. (Apart from the illustrations accompanying this article, other views of the station may be found in *SW24*.)

and the early railway companies were often reluctant to take any action to implement the recommendations of the Inspectors. The depressing truth is that railway staff were often left to struggle on with unsafe and primitive working practices until the death toll on the railways resulted in the Government passing legislation enforcing higher safety standards. Until then the travelling public and railway staff were left at greater risk than might otherwise be the case. One of the most significant pieces of legislation was the later Regulation of Railways Act 1889, which enabled the Board of Trade to enforce the implementation of block signalling, interlocking of points and signals, and continuous brakes on passenger trains, but this was many years in the future. Indeed it was this legislation that paved the way for the modern safe railways of the twentieth and twenty-first centuries.

Captain Tyler's Report

The official report by Captain H.W. Tyler of the circumstances surrounding this unfortunate incident gives an interesting insight into the operation of the early SER and the working lives of its employees in the early Victorian years. It concerns a head-on collision near Reading between a light engine leaving the locomotive depot on the wrong line and a down passenger train heading right line towards Reading from Wokingham. The account tells a story of an understaffed railway stretched to breaking point trying to cope with extra demands imposed by the running of excursion trains; of men being required to work excessive hours with minimal breaks; of a young and inexperienced boy having to work with poorly set up telegraph equipment; and of primitive and dangerous working practices, all of which combined to result in a dreadful accident. This account is set in the period when Charles Dickens was writing, and there is some resonance with his novels. Remember, he was a victim of the dreadful accident on the SER at Staplehurst a few years later (1865), which he survived, but it may well have contributed to his death in 1870.

The Reading Inquiry was conducted in two parts, initially on 19 September 1855 at Reading itself, and subsequently at London Bridge with evidence from Company officers on 16 and 19 October 1855.

The new terminus at Reading SER was manned by a stationmaster, three porters and a ticket collector. The rudimentary signalling that controlled the exit from the goods yard and engine shed was worked by one of the porters who would normally be engaged in duties at the station but on about ten occasions during the day would walk down the line to attend to the signal levers, which were located several hundred yards away near to the engine shed. At other times, the signals and points were left unattended or worked by the locomotive crews, in the main to control shunting movements, but not it should be noted, departures to Wokingham.

It was normal practice for the station staff to start work at 6am, and to finish at about 9.15pm, with three meal breaks totalling about two hours. On the day in question an excursion train had been arranged to run from Reading to Brighton (due to leave in two parts, the second departing at 9.00am), and

the stationmaster had to release three of his limited staff to help man the excursion, acting as guards. Consequently the stationmaster had to recruit the services of a temporary porter plus an unpaid relative approaching his 15th birthday to assist the remaining station staff. Together with the remaining porter, these men all worked from 6am until after 9pm and subsequently assisted through the night in clearing up the wreckage after the accident. All were examined in the subsequent inquiry. They were Benjamin Thew, stationmaster; William Sansom, porter; William Sayer, porter; and Charles Tarver, unpaid nephew of Benjamin Thew. All testified to the long hours of work, and the porters advised that on the day of the accident they had not been able to take their usual meal breaks because of the pressure of work. After the accident, the track clearance resulted in continuous work for these men for about twenty-four hours, virtually without sustenance during that time.

The inconvenient method of operation of the points and signals also meant that the locomotive crews were in the practice of setting the road in and out of the shed themselves, and they also regularly shunted past signals set at danger, an unacceptable practice, condemned by the Inspector. An early form of telegraph was in place that was intended to prevent more than one train in each direction occupying the same tracks between two adjoining block posts, and this was under the control of the stationmaster and his telegraph operator. The telegraph instrument remained in the original recently closed station, but the clock had been moved to the new station so there was a degree of guesswork on behalf of the staff in recording the time of messages. Naturally no train should leave Reading without the permission of either the stationmaster or the telegraph operator, but this was not what happened on the day of the accident.

The block section from Reading extended to Wokingham, and trains had to clear this section before a further service could be permitted to leave Reading. At about 6.15pm a telegraph message was received from Redhill requesting Reading to send a light engine to Guildford to meet the 6.30pm down train from Guildford, because the locomotive intended to work this train had to be taken to run one of the Brighton excursions. It appears that the Redhill telegraph operator had been trying to attract the attention of Reading for about an hour before the message was received, partly because of the staffing difficulties at Reading, and partly because the telegraph itself was not in good order. When the message was eventually received by Charles Tarver there was insufficient time to get a locomotive to Guildford, and something of a panic developed when a messenger (William Sansom) was dispatched to try and find Driver Joseph Crossley (who had gone home for a meal having worked a long shift) and get him to take an engine down to Guildford. By the time Crossley was located, it was after 7pm. Crossley made his way briskly to the engine shed, but could not locate his usual fireman, Edmund Christer, so he asked one of the cleaners, Jesse Ferguson to act as fireman. The engine was made ready in a rush, and Crossley instructed Ferguson to set the road and left the shed, running

Later BR days with 'G6' No 30277 seemingly in store outside Reading SR shed. Behind is the bulk of Reading East signal box and which clearly also shows the difference in levels between the SR and GWR lines. *Amyas Crump collection*

in reverse. Both men were still preoccupied in preparation work, the cleaner trimming lamps and the driver attending to the fire (this last statement might appear strange that the driver was so engaged, perhaps it was due to the junior nature of his 'mate') and filling his oil can, so neither of them noticed that the road had been wrongly set up (Up was Wokingham and Guildford, Down towards Reading) and that they were on the down line heading in the up direction. They left the shed without setting the signal to clear and without obtaining permission from the stationmaster.

Captain Tyler noted that some days earlier the up line had been in the possession of the engineers and temporary single-line working had been in force, and that Crossley may have thought this was still in force. The light engine was making good progress, when about 1½ miles out of Reading it met the 4.40pm down passenger train from London (via Redhill) travelling at about 40mph at 7.24pm. Neither crew was aware of the other train until it was far too late to stop, and the two met with considerable impact, killing five – four passengers and Joseph Crossley – and seriously injuring another ten. The Reading-bound train consisted of just four carriages and a brake van. Jesse Ferguson survived the accident, but was badly cut and gave his evidence in a statement from the Royal Berkshire Hospital, where he was still recovering from his injuries.

In looking at the circumstances of the accident, the inspector made it clear that although Driver Crossley's errors were apparent and that he was primarily to blame for the accident, the working practices of the SER were deplorable;

the points and signals should have been under the control of a signalman at all times; the SER should not have overworked its staff in the manner described, and should not have used station staff to substitute for other duties; there was inadequate supervision of the locomotive depot, which came under the sole authority of the stationmaster rather than being managed by a locomotive superintendent; more efficient arrangements should have been in place to locate drivers when they were required; and the telegraph should have been kept in better working order.

The one matter that the inspector commended the SER for was the use of the absolute block system for controlling trains, although it had failed to prevent this particular accident. Several railways, notably the SER's near neighbour, the London, Brighton and South Coast Railway, were particularly reluctant to replace the early practice of time interval working with the absolute block because it required investment in the electric telegraph, and the LB&SCR directors considered that reliance on the telegraph would result in staff being less vigilant, as they advised in considering the Inspector's report on the accident at Clayton Tunnel in 1861.

It is hard not to feel compassion for driver Crossley given the SER working practices of the time, and the official report makes it clear that the SER management needed to do better. Crossley had just completed a long shift and was not expecting to be called upon for further duties. All who gave evidence spoke of his good character and careful driving. It is impossible to know what frame of mind he was in when he set out on this additional duty, but in all probability he was tired after working a full shift, and he would also have been aware that they were running very late, and perhaps he simply cut corners in order not to cause further delay. Or was it just possible that the whole thing had a more sinister undercurrent, as will be considered later?

The Board of the SER, far from taking the Inspector's recommendations in hand, responded with a written rebuttal of his report, in which they impugned the integrity and impartiality of the Inspector. They took exception to the recommendation that there should be a full-time signalman on duty at all times by pointing out the low level of traffic on the line: five passenger and two freight trains daily. They compared working hours on the SER with employment on other railways and in the Metropolitan Police, where duties were longer and more onerous, and as a result considered a thirteen-hour working day to be entirely reasonable.

They pointed out the fact that the station staff being required to work throughout the following night was exceptional and solely due to the need to clear the line. At no point during this exchange was there any suggestion that any of the Inspector's recommendations would be acted upon. Consequently, it is not hard to spot an element of resentment in the attitude of the SER board in their response to the Board of Trade and its railway inspectors.

However, in the cold light of day it appears that some steps were taken to provide a switchman at the junction on a permanent basis, and to increase staffing levels at the station. These are both referred to as positive outcomes by Captain Tyler at the end of his report, which was issued on 14 November 1855. The report of the Inquiry, including a summary of the evidence presented to the Inspector, the Inspector's report, the subsequent correspondence between the SER board, the House of Lords and the Inspector's response, runs to a total of fifty-eight pages of close-printed text, so the issues were given a very full airing, more so than was the case with other accidents from the time where the reports can be quite brief.

Commentary

It is not easy at this distance in time to appreciate that the Victorian railways were at the pinnacle of technological achievement in their day. The development of the electric telegraph, for instance, offered an opportunity for a high degree of safety to be secured in the running of the railways. The first use on the railways took place in 1837 on the London and Birmingham Railway between Euston and Camden, and the Great Western Railway used the telegraph between Paddington and West Drayton in 1838. These installations were crude by later standards but paved the way for better systems to be developed. The SER remained in front of its rivals in this respect, especially during the middle years of the nineteenth century. The SER employed Charles Vincent Walker as its Signal and Telegraph Engineer and from 1852 the new technology was introduced across their system, using a system

of bell codes. Absolute block working was in force between Reading and Wokingham at the time of the accident.

Later, Walker designed block instruments that gave a visual indication of the state of the line, with some his equipment surviving in use from the 1860s until the 1960s even though they were quite outdated by then. He also designed a rotary train describer that helped signalmen to know what route approaching trains should take.

To us today the telegraph might have appeared to be very primitive in 1855, but it was not far from cutting edge technology and it was instead the undisciplined operation of the railway signalling at Reading that led directly to the accident.

At this time, the concentration of the control of points and signals within signal boxes was not usual, and signalmen attended to their operation using levers attached directly to the individual points and signals. The widespread installation of signal boxes having lever operating signals and points in a set area did not start until the 1860s. By the 1870s the Board of Trade was pressuring the railways to use the absolute block system of train control, which relied on the use of the electric telegraph, with signal and line control concentrated in the signal box. In 1889, legislation made the use of the absolute block compulsory in Great Britain and Ireland. Had there been proper control of the signals and points together with a rigorous operational discipline then it is unlikely that the tragic accident that took place outside Reading on 12 September 1855 would have occurred, notwithstanding the long working hours to which the staff were subjected, but this was still some way in the future.

Captain Tyler later conceded that the lengthy continuous time at work in this case was caused in part by the occurrence of the accident and that this was exceptional. He did not exonerate the SER for their approach to employment, and made the point that the degree of mismanagement and disregard for the safety of the travelling public exhibited by the SER exceeded anything previously reported to the House of Lords. As for Joseph Crossley, he was reported to be a man of good character, steady, sober and quiet. He had been on the railway for ten years, having progressed from cleaner to engine driver. He had been promoted to fireman eight years before, and had been a driver for three years. The Inspector struggled to understand how he could have not been aware that they were on the wrong line. His explanation that the line to Wokingham had been singled for some time beforehand and Crossley may have thought that wrong line working was still in force is the best he could come up with, but is it credible? The special working had ended thirteen days earlier, and Crossley had on the same day already run two trains out of Reading – *on the normal line*.

As an aside, Captain Tyler made some comments on the braking power available on the excursion trains. Referring to an accident inquiry in 1854 at Croydon over which he had presided, he had then advised the SER to provide one brake for every seven carriages. He noted that in the Reading case one of the excursion trains contained twenty-eight carriages, yet only two brakes were provided, and the line ran over gradients as steep as 1 in 93. Noting that excursion trains were usually heavily loaded, he reminded the Company of his 1854 recommendations, and reprimanded it for ignoring them so soon afterwards. This is long before the availability of automatic continuous brakes, and again points to the railway's cost-cutting attitude, putting profit before the safety of passengers and staff. The prospect of a fully loaded excursion train of twenty-eight carriages attempting to climb Gomshall bank with the small, light locomotives of the period, and then controlling the descent towards Dorking with perhaps a 200-ton tail load conjures up an interesting picture. Not least we may presume banking or piloting assistance would have been necessary.

Extracts from the Evidence of the Fireman

Some of the reported evidence is particularly poignant; Jesse Ferguson, the engine cleaner who stood in as fireman, gave evidence from his bed in the Royal Berkshire Hospital. His evidence was taken by the Coroner, not the Inspector. (Today this sounds not a little macabre. Did he actually survive or was this what might be better known now as a 'dying declaration'?) If it seems somewhat repetitive, allowances should be made for the injuries he suffered, which were described by the driver of the Reading bound train, William Graham, who also gave his evidence from his bed in the same hospital as follows: 'I found the fireman of the other engine in a corner of the footplate of his own engine, very much cut about the face, we laid him on the bank.' Ferguson stated that, 'I was an engine cleaner on the South Eastern Railway at Reading, and occasionally employed as a stoker. I was so employed as stoker in the evening of Wednesday last, the 12 September instant, when Francis Croke told me a telegraphic message had been received for an engine to go to Guildford to meet the express train, and that I was to prepare the engine immediately. I prepared the engine accordingly, and I knew it was Crossley's engine. The person who cleans the engine when the fireman or stoker is not there has to go. I accordingly went.

'When the deceased Crossley came, he told me to jump up, and to trim the lamps which I proceeded to do. The one in front of the engine was lighted, that at the back was not lighted. I was occupied in trimming the lamps, and was going to light them, when the concussion took place. The lamps should have been lighted before we left the station. The engine was running backwards and the end lamp was not lighted. Before we started I suggested that the lamps should be lighted, but Crossley said, we will light them before we get to Wokingham – so implying they would either pause en route or more likely one of them would walk over the tender or around the framing whilst the engine was in motion. The deceased Crossley was guiding, and had command of the engine. My duties as stoker were to see that there was a good fire, light the lamps and mind the break (sic). We started at about half past seven in the evening (but I don't know exactly) from the engine house at Reading station, and I did not perceive on which line of rails we were, as I was engaged in cleaning the lamps. It might occupy about ten minutes in

'U' No 31862 awaiting departure bound for Redhill in 1964. By this time there were four platform faces at Reading (Southern). With rebuilding of the former GWR station in recent years a photograph attempted from this same standpoint today would either be impossible due to redevelopment but also create a totally different vista. *Amyas Crump collection*

getting from the station to the place where the concussion took place. On our going along the road, Crossley made the observation that we should only be able to get as far as Ashe *(sic)*, as we should not have time to get to Guildford. I do not know on what line of rails we went; we should not have gone on the down line of rail. In the case of ordinary trains, it is the duty of the switchman to arrange the points; but in the case of a pilot engine, as in this case, in the absence of a switchman, the driver orders the fireman to get down and hold the points. In this case Crossley said nothing to me about the points – he merely asked me to jump up, and we went off rather fast. Crossley, during our journey up the line, looked at the fire, and poured out the oil for oiling the engine and tender. I was aware, and so was Crossley, that a train was expected about that time; I cannot at all account for his being on the down line of rails. The lights approaching the down train were not lighted. I believe the signals at the sidings going into the engine-shed were standing at danger; they generally stand so when a train is not expected. Some minute or two before the concussion took place, the cylinder cocks were shut and we were blowing off steam from the dome. The approaching train could not hear the blowing off the steam, and I think our engine could not be seen by them.'

The Search for Crossley

Joseph Crossley went off duty after arriving at Reading at 5pm with the 2.22pm train from Redhill. On the search to find driver Crossley, here is the evidence of the porter, William Sansom: 'The telegraph boy, Charles Tarver, who was the only person with me at the station, gave me the message about twenty-five or twenty minutes past six. I said, Mr Thew has left me in charge of the office, I can't go; you had better take it to the engine driver. He said, "I have got my work, and can't go." I said, "if you don't go, you must stop and take charge of the office." He did not seem willing to do either. At last, I persuaded him to take it to Mr Thew, who had gone to tea. The boy came back and said to me, "You'll have to go if I can't find one of the cleaners." He went to the shed to find a cleaner, but couldn't and brought the message back. I went with it at once, as fast as I could run, to the engine driver's house. I saw a driver, Crook, but he could not tell me where Crossley lived. I enquired in the goods shed of Mr Norton, who told me the direction, but couldn't say exactly. I then ran to the "Cannon" public house. They said they didn't know. I then went to the "Spotted Dog". They told me. I saw a female at his house who called him and told him he had to go. I gave him the message. He was perfectly sober, and very collected, and said he would go directly. He asked the time of the female, who said it was past seven, and I said yes, he has got no time to spare. As I was coming from the door the church clock struck seven. He had asked me to tell his mate, in passing the shed, to stir up the fire and get ready. I did so. After that, I came to the station, and began lighting my lamps. After lighting them, I went to the office, where I found the station-master. I told him that I had found Crossley, who would "be here directly". It was more than a quarter-past seven.'

Working Hours

Porters Sansom and William Sayer also had something to say about their working hours: Sansom – 'All the porters left at the station were at work from six in the morning until four the next morning on that day after the accident.' 'I always begin work at 6am and leave off about 10 minutes or a quarter past 9. I generally have forty minutes for breakfast, an hour for dinner, and half, or three-quarters of an hour for tea. All the other porters have the same hours for work.' 'When we were at the other station, one of us left work every third week at six, but that has been given up since we have been at the new station. We are supposed also to have one Sunday out of three, but I have been on four Sundays, at the same hours as on weekdays.' 'I am hardworked between all the trains every day. I am awkwardly situated at the new station, with regard to my lamps and tools.' 'I think we are worked harder than we ought to be in length of time.'

Sayer added, 'I came on duty at a quarter-past 5am on 12 September, and first got away at 11. I did not get anything to eat until 11, except a piece of bread and cheese I put in my pocket in the morning at starting. I did not go off duty at all that night or the next morning. At 9am on the 12th, I felt a little queer, and I wanted to go home, but the station-master persuaded me to stop, because the other men had not come. Sansom was ill, and Sullivan had gone guard with an ordinary passenger train.' 'I have worked the last three or four Sundays the same hours as on weekdays, because one or two of the men have been ill. The work is rather hard, and it is rather too long a time.'

The Unpaid Telegraph Operator

Charles Tarver, the 14-year-old nephew of station master Benjamin Thew who was working unpaid, was also called to testify. He was clearly proud of having learnt to use the electric telegraph. On the face of it, unpaid employment sounds somewhat alarming, but Benjamin Thew explained later that he was training this boy to take a paid position on the railway. His youthfulness is apparent in the report of his evidence: 'I have been about four months at the station and began learning the telegraph immediately. I can read it perfectly now, and have been able to do so for a fortnight or three weeks. I do not get anything for it from the Company.' 'At a quarter past six on the 12th September, I received a message to tell Crossley to go and meet the 6.30 train from London at Guildford. I went to Sansom, and he couldn't leave the station. I then went to Mr Thew, who said a cleaner was to take the message to Crossley. I went to the shed, and could not find a cleaner, so Sansom took the message.' 'For the last three weeks, I have been employed every day for some time in the day, to attend to the instrument and keep the books. When the instrument calls Reading, whoever is near it attends to it, that is to say, the ticket-collector, me, or Mr Thew. Whoever attends to the instrument makes the entry in the book.' 'There is no clock in the telegraph office, and when the accident occurred, and for three or four days before, I could not tell what o'clock it was when I received messages. A clock has now been put on the platform at the new station.' 'The telegraph was at the old station at the time of the accident, and I had no clock then, because it was moved up to the new station.' 'I used then to take every message to Mr Thew, and at the same time to look at the clock at the new station. The signal book and clock were both at the new station for three or four days, whilst the telegraph was at the old station.' 'I may have made several entries in the book by guess-work, but I cannot say I have, or remember when I did it, except on that evening.' 'I was fourteen years old last October.'

A Mystery in Passing

We have briefly encountered William Graham, the driver of the Reading-bound train who tended to the injured fireman, Jesse Ferguson. In his evidence, he was reported to have had thirty years' experience on steam locomotives. If this was correct, that would have meant that he had started in 1825, and it begs the question as to where he was so early in the railway age. I think it is likely that the record is incorrect; perhaps the clerk to the Inquiry misheard, and Graham said that he had started thirteen years before, which would

coincide with the opening of part of the SER line east of Redhill in 1842. After all, 1825 marked the opening of the pioneering Stockton and Darlington Railway, and was five years before the opening of the Canterbury and Whitstable and ten years before the London and Greenwich.

The Big Cheeses at London Bridge

As well as taking evidence from the staff directly involved with the operation of the railway at Reading, Captain Tyler also heard a number of the senior officers of the SER. This hearing took place about a month later at London Bridge, and was also attended by several of the Company Directors. Amongst those giving evidence were Captain R.H. Barlow; General Manager; G.W. Brown, Superintendent; and James Cudworth, Locomotive Superintendent. Some of the individuals who had earlier appeared before Captain Tyler in Reading were called back to give further evidence. It is clear from this evidence that there was considerable friction amongst the Officers, particularly between Barlow and Brown.

Barlow started his evidence by explaining that he had been dismissed by the Company on the day of the Inquiry, and spent a great deal of time complaining about how he had been

Looking the other way and this time it is 'Class 4' No 76066 that waits to leave. By this time the engine shed was beyond the station on the left but, as can be seen from the early plan, it had originally been on the opposite side of the line. Reading gas works is in the distance, whilst nearby had been the Huntley & Palmer's biscuit factory, which operated its own small fleet of locomotives. *Amyas Crump collection*

sidelined and had not been kept informed of matters concerning the running of the Company. Such undisguised friction could not have been conducive to the smooth running of the railway. There was a significant amount of evidence given in respect of savings that the railway was making by downgrading staff and reducing the number of porters across the entire railway. Barlow and Brown clearly disagreed about this policy, Barlow considering that the reductions were having a detrimental effect on the running of the railway. Indeed it transpires that the company had reduced the total number of porters across the system by eighteen in the previous six months. A report dated 16 August 1855 by the Superintendent, Engineer and Goods Manager is appended to the papers from the Inquiry, in which the savings at Reading are listed. Three posts were affected; the ticket collector was to be superseded by a youth, reducing the weekly wage bill from 21 shillings to 12 shillings; the same saving was to be achieved by dispensing with an assistant goods clerk and employing another youth; and the horse keeper's services were to be dispensed with altogether. The annual savings from these staff changes totalled about £86.

The Officers praised the readiness of the station master at Reading to propose reductions, although the Officers stated that they were of the opinion that their stations were already worked economically. I am not quite sure what to make of this. Maybe the Company had offered some sort of incentive to its station masters to suggest economies? The account of the day-to-day running of the railway suggests that the staff at Reading were under severe pressure, and the station master must have been aware of the difficulties in finding enough staff to operate properly, so why would he feel the downgrading of his staff was a good idea? In his further evidence, Thew gives some explanation. The assistant goods clerk then in post was in line for promotion elsewhere, and he was lining up his nephew to replace the ticket collector following a period of unpaid training. The position of horse keeper was said to contribute nothing to the running of the station and his services could be dispensed with.

James Cudworth also gave evidence. He was in post as Locomotive Superintendent for a lengthy period from 1845 and, after some early experimentation, standardised the locomotive stock of the SER, until eventual interference by Sir Edward Watkin in locomotive design put him in an intolerable position and he resigned in 1876. He advised that on the day of the accident, Crossley had started work at about 6.30am carrying out some shunting before taking the 9.00am excursion to Guildford. He returned with the locomotive to Reading, then ran the 12.15pm to Redhill, returning with the 2.22pm, which arrived at Reading at about 5pm. He did not consider that this was particularly onerous, notwithstanding the additional duty in the evening. There is no description in the report of the locomotives involved in the accident, apart from the light engine having a tender and running in reverse. The Reading line was treated as something of a backwater, so in all probability the locomotives would have been early types.

Conclusion

The Railway Company refuted most of the recommendations of Captain Tyler, but he was able to report that by the date of his report a switchman was kept permanently at the junction, and that the staff of the Reading passenger station had been increased by two porters. Captain Tyler expressed the hope, probably somewhat forlornly, that the Company would increase staffing levels over the remainder of the line. In reading through the Inquiry papers, the circumstances surrounding this unfortunate accident come into sharper focus; the long hours that were the norm for the hard-pressed staff; the stresses caused by losing porters to provide guards for excursion trains; the unfortunate delay in picking up the telegraph message requiring an engine to be sent off to Guildford; the panic-stricken search for a driver to take the engine out in the evening, bordering on farce; the rush to get on the road after the unfortunate delay; the inexplicable decision by Crossley to set out on the wrong road. As with all accident accounts, there is an excruciating inevitability as the story unfolds. If only the telegraph had been efficiently operating and properly attended, how much time might have been saved? With the extra time, might Crossley have been more careful in setting the road, or maybe reporting to Thew for clearance to go? And crucially, what if Crossley or Ferguson had realised that they were on the wrong line? There are other little glimpses into day-to-day life; catching the chimes of the church clock, or simply using guesswork to work out the time of day, for instance, as certainly not all workers in that era could afford a pocket watch.

The one matter over which the SER ought to receive credit was the speed with which it introduced block signalling across its network. In this one respect it was streets ahead of some of its rivals. Perhaps this is why Charles Vincent Walker (Signal and Telegraph Engineer) was not summoned to appear at the Inquiry; he was already doing an excellent job. He had first introduced a simple telegraph in 1852, and by 1861 virtually the entire SER system was equipped with it.

Charles Dickens' last novel, unfinished when he died, was *The Mystery of Edwin Drood*. Dickens took the solution of Drood's disappearance with him to the grave. The Reading accident could more imaginatively be entitled *The Mystery of Joseph Crossley*. Captain Tyler's best effort at explaining why he set off on the wrong line does not entirely ring true. By 7.15 or 7.30pm in mid-September the light would not have been good – there was no British Summer Time – but it would probably have been adequate for Crossley to realise he was on the wrong line; and he would probably have been aware that a train running towards Reading was due. Perhaps his state of mind was not as collected as testimonials suggest; perhaps fatigue had muddled his thinking; or, darkest of all, perhaps his actions were deliberate. It is understandable that the Inspector would not have voiced such dark thoughts when the accident was so recent and had such a tragic outcome. Crossley's actions in starting off without setting the line; without confirming orders from the station master; and without having the locomotive properly prepared and lit suggest that this might have been the

The later Reading (Southern) station, recorded in the mid to late 1960s – we automatically tend to look at the cars from the period: 1100, A40, Zephyr, etc. Alongside is the 'Road and Rail Travel Bureau', which manifests itself today as the coach connecting Reading with Heathrow. What a wonderful enamel sign on the end nearest the camera.

case, but it does not tie with the witnesses' character testimonies. There was a major panic going on that clouded clear thinking. His fireman appears to have been so absorbed with preparing the lamps to the extent that he testified that he was not aware of which line they were running along. Only Joseph Crossley could have known what was on his mind, and he took this with him when he died.

Appendix – According to 'Bradshaw' for March 1850, passenger services left Reading for Wokingham and beyond at 7.45 and 10.50am, and 12.30, 2.50 and 6.50pm. In the opposite direction, passenger trains arrived at Reading at 10.45am, 12.15, 1.45, 4.45 and 7.20pm. In addition, there were two freight trains each way, but of course these are not listed in Bradshaw. The timings of services do not seem to have changed a great deal by 1855.

Reference – A copy of the original accident enquiry, fifty-eight pages, is available to view at: www.railwaysarchive.co.uk/documents/BoT_Reading1855.pdf

Terry Cole's Rolling Stock Files No 40
Any Colour as Long as it's Red

There has been some discussion in the model railway world as to whether the BR crimson livery used by Messrs Bachmann, and also by Messrs Hornby on their respective 'Birdcage' sets and 'LSWR non-corridor coaches', is indeed the right shade of red. Colour, after all, is something on which we can all have an opinion. Now determining the colour of something is difficult in any event, let alone at more than half a century distant, and is perhaps best summarised as being 'subjective'. Whatever, the perceived colour depends on the light, from how far away it is viewed, and how much of the colour there actually is. Then we have the question of what paint and what undercoat was used, how much the colour has faded and how dirty the paintwork is. It is also unlikely that the various railway workshops used the same recipe. Western Region red, for example, always appeared as a more strident and orangey colour compared to the Southern. Was Lancing red the same as Eastleigh red or Ryde red, and was it the same red as was used with 'cream' on corridor coaches? Possibly not, since the 'all-red livery' was described as unlined crimson

and the other carmine and cream. It certainly didn't look the same but colour photographs of the period can be unreliable due to deterioration of the emulsion used. However, photos are all we have to go on, so here goes!

If you would like to research this further there are a number of 1950s colour photographs in *'The Premier Collection, 1950s and 1960s Southern Steam in Colour'* published by Crecy.

This photo of A1x No 377S on a special train is taken at Kemp Town on 3 November 1956. We get a good view of ex-LBSC push-pull set No 650, which looks as if it has very recently been painted. Indeed the red almost seems to match the vermilion panel in the centre of the buffer beam and is therefore more akin to 'buffer beam red'. Certainly it appears brighter than the Hornby or Bachmann coaches. Set No 650 comprises an ex-LBSCR arc-roofed coach converted in 1931 to Driving Brake Composite No 6940 and an ex-LBSCR 48ft Third Trailer.

This nice picture of 'Birdcage' set No 520 is at an unknown location and taken probably in the early to middle 1950s. Unfortunately the slide has acquired a reddish hue with age, which makes colour matching difficult. However, the red appears much duller and closer to the colour of the Bachmann models.

This is probably as good as it gets in determining the colour of a particular coach. This lovely 'Kodachrome 1' slide (a very stable and colour correct film) was taken at Ventnor definitely in the first half of the 1950s – we can date it as the locomotive, the elusive W15 *Cowes,* was withdrawn in June 1956. We get a good look at the red on ex-LBSCR brake No S4170S and also on the ex-LBSCR saloon coach seen in the background, Ryde being renowned for keeping its vintage rolling stock looking immaculate. The red on the coach, although very fresh, does show some traffic staining but again is noticeably darker and appears quite close to the Hornby LSWR red. So are the models currently being produced too dark? Possibly a tad, but I'm not going to be repainting mine anytime soon. Instead I am just going to enjoy some exquisite models. I rest my case!

For this chapter in the archive we are able to call upon something additional to the available images. As many will know, 'SCT' was an enthusiast as well as being a professional and he was keen to both inform and entertain others through the pages of the *Meccano Magazine* (for boys). We will see his writing later under his own name but for the moment it appears under the pseudonym 'Shedmaster' but he also later used the term 'Shed Superintendent. A number of his views also appear to have been taken to illustrate specific articles and, whilst ideal for the purpose, sixty-odd years later they also serve as a window into the general scene of the period, something that could never have been perceived at the time.

Driver's eye view – well, pretty close, anyway. Taken from the leading guard's van looking ahead to the (unidentified) 'Merchant Navy' heading, we think, towards Waterloo. Certainly it is on a four-track section and the lines are electrified, so at a guess it could be the cutting east of Byfleet. This was one of four, almost identical, images all taken in a similar area but the only one to have the driver leaning out. For those not familiar with the restricted view presented from the Bulleid cab here is a good example of the difficulties faced by the driver.

The *Meccano Magazine* for 1947 carried two articles by 'SCT' under the pseudonym 'Shed Superintendent'. Each of was one page and included illustrations, most of which can now be seen again more than seventy years later. The first, in the January issue, was entitled 'Station by the Sea':

The Isle of Wight is a mecca for railway enthusiasts in the South. You need go no further than Ryde Pier Head to observe many unusual features. On stepping off the steamer, you find yourself at a railway terminus nearly half-a-mile out to sea! In rough weather the waves lash uncomfortably close to the carriage floor, and the sensations of the visitors are very different from the atmosphere of smoke and drabness which surrounds a city terminus. At Ryde Pier Head the engines are given attention between trains, the nearest locomotive depot being some way away on the other side of the town. A water main runs along the pier to a tank situated off the end of the middle platform, and to take water the fireman stands on the engine framing, controlling the water valve by pulling a wire. All the Island engines are tanks, there being four E1s, three A1Xs, and twenty O2s, so that no provision is made for a turntable.

When ashpans or smokeboxes have to be cleaned, the ashes are disposed of by the simple method of dropping then through holes in the flooring to the sea, and drivers have to be careful when oiling their engines that they, too, do not take an involuntary bathe! The station has a complete loudspeaker system, and arriving steamers are greeted with a cheery 'Good Morning' followed by details of the next trains, and altogether the impression made by this unusual terminus is a pleasant start to an Island holiday.

Below and overleaf: **Aside from the first photograph of this series depicting the general railway scene from the ferry, the following three views accompanied the article. What we do not know, of course, is if this a form of pleasure trip to obtain images for the article or it was for some other purpose. Certainly on this occasion few images seem to have been taken. Did the young fireman emptying the smokebox of No 15 *Cowes* have any idea who was taking his photograph?**

The single firing image used to accompany the article was one of no fewer than sixteen similar views. We can say with certainty the footplate is a Bulleid and the photograph has also been carefully arranged – notice the lighting, not burning coals – in the firebox. We also know that a few years later an official booklet on controlled firing techniques was produced by the newly formed British Railways with some of the illustrations coming from the SCT stable.

A few months later, in July 1947, a second, unrelated, piece appeared in the same magazine and again using the same pseudonym. This time the title was, 'Have you ever thought about this? What kind of shovel does a Fireman use?' We should recall of course the *MM* was aimed primarily at a younger audience and was thus written in such a context. With slightly more text this time, just two views were used and it is to be regretted that we have not been able to source the original of the second image referred to showing a large number of shovels awaiting repair:

Could you draw a fireman's shovel from memory? I should not be surprised if some readers sketched something like a garden spade at their first attempt. As a matter of fact, firing a locomotive requires a shovel of special shape. A good fireman is as particular about his shovel as a tennis player is about a racquet. The shovel must be well-balanced and of exactly the right length. The metal part – known as the blade – is almost as long as the shaft, as can be seen from the photographs. The blade is 1ft 8in (50cm) long. These shovels are made by two or three well-known manufacturers, and special steel is used for the blades to withstand the wear incurred in scooping up each shovelful of coal. For this purpose the leading edge of the blade must be kept sharp. A deep rim round the edge of the shovel prevents coal falling off with the motion of the engine, the lumps being about the size of a man's fist for the best results.

The shaft is made of hard wood, without any tendency to splinter, as the fireman slides one hand down the shaft at each stroke of firing. The shaft is topped by a tee-piece which is firmly gripped in the fireman's other hand – either right or left according to the side of the engine from which the fireman works. The tee-piece forms a safeguard against the shovel slipping out of the fireman's hands into the firebox! This has happened more than once and has compelled him to use his bare hands until the next stopping place. In fact, a train on one occasion stopped specially at a wayside station with the fireman sent off to the porters' room to borrow a scuttle-shovel! Some fireman cut their shovel-blades to a narrow shape, to give more clearance with the firehole door. Others set the blade to a particular angle with the shaft, to suit the length of arm, as this naturally governs the angle at which the coal shoots off the shovel into the firebox. An average shovelful of coal weighs twenty pounds, and on a journey of 200 miles the fireman will make about 800 strokes, at the rate of some seven shovelfuls every two minutes. In course of time the blade becomes worn down at the leading edge and becomes too short for further use. These worn shovels are then collected at a central depot for re-blading, as illustrated. If a hot meal is required, a well-polished shovel also makes an excellent frying pan. When placed inside the firehole door for a few moments, eggs and bacon can be cooked to a turn! This is seldom done nowadays for obvious reasons!

(The reasons won't be obvious today – but it was all to do with rationing, of course.)

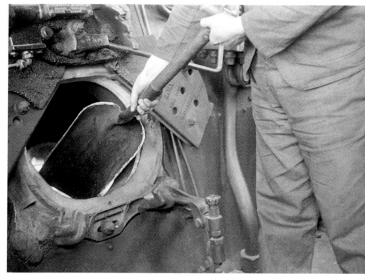

At the same time as the firing views were taken, SCT also recorded a number of other images along a similar theme, based partly on footplate duties but also with the titles, 'How to look at an injector, and how to get underneath safely'. Again, some of these featured in the later instructional book and might even be considered to form an early type of 'Health & Safety'. No names for any of the participants are given.

Next time in this feature: A Portsmouth electric divided at Woking, Ministry of Transport inspection on the Isle of Wight, two special trains, a broken tyre on a 'King Arthur', and the 'Bournemouth Belle' makes an unscheduled stop at Byfleet.

Right and overleaf: **Finally for this issue, three images consequent upon an incident of buffer locking at Richmond in 1946–47. We are given limited details: 'Small NE van and large GW vehicle'.**

Rebuilt
The Letters and Comments Pages

With sincere apologies to Alan Postlethwaite, this particular image was omitted from his recent 'Exeter-Plymouth' article in *SW41*. Headed by D2176, an up freight passes through St Budeaux (Victoria Road). The down starting signals are: L&SWR Main Line (left), GWR Main Line (centre) and an industrial branch (right). This connection to the GWR gave the L&SWR access to the RN Dockyard at Devonport. In 1964, the L&SWR main line closed between here and Devonport Junction. The line north to Bere Alston remains open to this day for Gunnislake trains.
Bluebell Archives, John J. Smith collection, 1962

We start this issue with a small bit of reminiscing from the Editor. A few weeks ago I was enjoying lunch with long-standing friend Peter Squibb. Peter is a retired railwayman and a superb modeller who easily puts my own efforts to shame. Now fear not, I am not about to start telling about the menu or the service but I will repeat a few little stories recounted during the course of the meal. Peter is a fount of stories (see also *SW* issues, 7, 14 and 19), but a few more will not, I am sure go amiss.

The first was in the days when men working on the ground were first told they must wear hard hats (as well as other items of 'health and safety' clothing). Several men were sent to a site, the purpose of which is irrelevant. Well, one of these simply tripped on the ballast and ended up lying prone. He was not injured – then at least – and was in the process of getting himself up when up rushes another shouting, 'Don't move, don't move – I have done a first-aid course'. It made no difference that our friend on the ground had simply tripped and was perfectly alright – as indeed he was until the helmet of our first-aider slipped off his head and dropped peak first on to the temple of the one of the ground – knocking him out …

Still dealing with ballast, we come to the time the linemen's office received a call to say that the signalman at Box 'A' had lost all communication with 'Box 'B' – block/bells the lot. The linemen immediately knew what was likely, as a complete failure of everything invariably meant the theft of the copper telegraph wires; as was indeed a regular occurrence in an area that was notorious for a certain type of community. (Political correctness prevents me from being more specific.) Anyway, a posse of linemen set forth (is that the correct noun or might it even be a 'cable' of linemen …?) and it was soon apparent that theft was indeed the cause. Whereupon the British Transport Police arrived, insisting nothing was touched or moved until they had gathered forensic evidence in the hope of identifying the perpetrators. The suggestion was made that they start by fingerprinting the ballast …

Finally, the tale of the poor swan. This occurred in the area of Poole and involved a swan that managed to create its own demise by flying into telegraph wires nearby, thereby breaking either the communication or block circuit between two adjacent signal boxes. When this type of failure occurred there was no option but to walk along the pole route until the break was found and it was not long before the cause was located. Fortunately no wires had been severed by the swan and the two linemen involved managed to cure the problem simply by pushing and prodding the now lifeless bird until it was dislodged and fell to the ground. With no short circuit now apparent, normal service was promptly resumed. As it was out of hours they also claimed overtime. Now the problem was these two had long been suspected of perhaps being a little over-enthusiastic with their claims and this latest one, 'Swan caused communication failure', was the final straw to S & T management at Salisbury, who were then the overseers of Poole. The trouble was though that since the closure of the direct line south from Salisbury via Fordingbridge, any management attempts to catch them out involved a train journey via Southampton and so there was plenty of notice available to Poole that 'trouble was on the way'. Salisbury, though, decided to call their bluff and insisted on evidence before they would authorise the claim. Poole responded, venturing out to collect what was by now a rather 'ripe' specimen before sealing it in a crate and despatching it to Salisbury. One can only imaging the reaction of the office at Salisbury upon opening their parcel. Poole got their overtime paid.

SW41 – BR Renumbering and *Ellerman Line*

We start properly with a note from Stuart Hicks. '*SW41* is another interesting read thank you, particularly the Littlehampton shipping article that I have been reading recently. Recall we were recently discussing the trials with LMS 2-6-4T No 42199... ' Stuart suggests that as this was in 1948, the Derby visit (p.79) may well have been to effect a number change from 2199 to 42199 – a perfectly feasible suggestion as well.

He adds, on an unrelated topic, that the original GWR and indeed its successors even to this day use the term 'relief lines' in preference to the LSW term 'local' line, or more generally 'slow line' (p.81). We may indeed wonder how many other terms harking back sixty or seventy years or more are still in place that are railway- or region-specific. Finally, one the Editor must apologise for, a slip of the finger meant the sectioned (dismembered might be a better term) 'Merchant Navy' at York was identified as 35019, it should, of course, be 35029.

SW35 – Yet more on the Demise of No 35004

We were approached recently by Southampton man Dave Harman. As a young man Dave, together with a friend, happened to be on the train hauled by No 35004 when it came to grief. (Quite amazing what still turns up on the subject.) Dave recalls they were in the front passenger coach travelling at a reasonable speed when there was a crunching sound followed immediately by ballast flying past the carriage window. The train then came to a fairly rapid halt. On looking out of the window he could see 'something sticking out from the side' of the engine and either the driver or fireman on the ground examining this. He recalls that whilst stopped they were given no information from anyone – the guard certainly did not walk through the train – and the next they knew was when after no more than thirty minutes they were being hauled back to Basingstoke 'wrong road'.

No 35004, as we know, remained where she was until attended to by fitters later. Upon arrival at Basingstoke, there did not appear to be any more information available to passengers, certainly not when they might be able to continue their journey, so both continued to what was their intended destination in London, travelling via Reading and the WR. Dave recalls visiting Eastleigh a few days later and finding No 35004 in the well-known spot with tender detached but separated by only a few feet. As we know, the tender was subsequently reused but that was the end for No 35004. Looking at this half a century later, and regardless of the inaction of the guard in informing passengers, all credit must be given to the railwaymen in firstly advising the signalman – control of their predicament, Basingstoke finding another engine at very short notice, and the issue of /signing distribution of 'wrong line' orders for the passenger train to be hauled back to Basingstoke 'wrong road'. We would still love to see the internal report on the incident if anyone knows where such might be found. It was not the subject of a Ministry enquiry.

Graham Biggles with a Question on Locomotive Classification

One now for the experts. 'What does the number '15' refer to when it comes to the various LSWR/SR classes: 'D15', 'H15', 'N15', 'S15' etc? Perhaps the whole subject of class designations might be worthy of some elaboration if someone could assist?' Graham also asks a teaser, 'In its lifetime, the SE&CR never named its locos but there was one that did later bear a name for a time after the company had ceased and became part of the Southern Railway; do you know which one?" (The answer is in illustration later in this section.) (Alastair Wilson also knew the answer to this one without

---

Opposite and overleaf: **Connecting with the current 'Rolling Stock Files' in this issue, we have pleasure in adding three additional views of red coaches from the archive of Trevor Owen. They show the 5 October 1957 'Compass Rose' special organised by the Railway Enthusiasts Club, at Godalming old station (Godalming Goods). This tour commences at the home location of the REC, Farnborough, at 1.36pm, and on the outward trip took the route: Farnborough-Sturt Lane West Junc.-Frimley Junc.-Frimley- Frimley Junc.-Ash Vale-Aldershot North Junc.-Aldershot Government Sidings Station-Aldershot North Junc.-Aldershot East Junc.-Ash Junc.-Wanborough-Ash Junc.-Tongham-Ash Junc.-Wanborough-Guildford-Shalford Junc.-Farncombe and Godalming Goods. The return was Godalming Goods- Farncombe-Shalford Junc.-Guildford-Woking Junc.-Byfleet & New Haw-Addlestone Junc.-Chertsey (via the Virginia Water west curve)-Sunningdale-Ascot-Wokingham-New Junc.- Reading General- Southcote Junction.-Reading Central Goods-Southcote Junc.- Reading West-Southcote Junc.-Bramley-Basingstoke-Thornycroft's siding-Basingstoke and Farnborough, where arrival was just two minutes late at 7.57pm. (Itinerary thanks to www.sixbellsjunction.co.uk). 'M7' No 30051 was used throughout with two-coach pull-push set No 721.**

seeing the illustration. | He also adds, 'In the strictest of terms, Graham is correct – but one of Stirling's F class (No. 40?) bore the name *Onward* or *Forward* when it was exhibited in Paris in 1880 – but I don't think it carried the name on to SECR days.)

A follow-up to the Locomotive Exchanges by the Author, Jeremy Clarke in *SW38*

Exchange trials. 'Hi Kevin, thought this might interest you. I have been going through the mountain of magazines I've acquired over the years and found something of relevance to this in the 20th Anniversary Special of *Trains Illustrated* (NOT we hasten to add the Ian Allan publication, which by this time had become *Modern railways* anyway'). It's also emblazoned "Steam Alive". I can't find a publishing date but it's priced at 3/6 and some of the book costs noted in the advertising inside make me salivate. But I digress, an article on the "Black 5" is the one that, to a degree, further convinces me the LMR enginemen were under orders to keep coal and water consumption down and hang the timetable.

'It is written by someone who is obviously an LMR engineer under the pseudonym "45671" and concerns his being required to find out why a batch of "Black 5s" built at Horwich displayed rough riding, heavy axle-box knock and liveliness absent from other members of the class. He recounts a shocking trip from Glasgow to Perth with No 4797 and a return with No 4789 that was just as bad. After a lot of investigation it was determined the valve settings were wrong, proved by a subsequent most superb trip with the same No 4789 when this had been attended to.

'With "5" No 45253 selected for the trials it was transferred to Kentish Town and a test run made with an Inspector on board. This showed the engine had all the bad traits of the others of the batch. Accordingly the valves were reset to the proper standards and another test made. The author concedes a very skilled crew and supervising Inspector were on the footplate besides himself. Ten bogies were brought from York to St Pancras with several stops on the way. The skill was shown in that the pressure was always between 215 and 225lb against a continually working injector, no smoke and not once did the safety valves lift. And she rode beautifully. Consumption worked out at 21.8 gallons per mile, equivalent he estimates to about 30lb of coal. Now comes the interesting bit, and I quote: "... to this economy there is no doubt that expert firemanship, high superheat due to an incandescent fire and skilled driving all contributed. After that, what a miserable exhibition of effort-saving and bad time-keeping was given with such an excellent machine in the exchange trials! Any resemblance between, say, the performances between Marylebone and Manchester and what a class "5" *could* do was purely accidental". Could one find anything more condemning that that?'

From Chris Sayer-Leavy (*SW38/SW40*) etc, and A816

'Good morning Kevin, I am rather in catch-up mode here, but I would like to extend my thanks to John Harvey (*SW40*

Rebuilt, p.92) for reminding me of Holcroft's comments on the A816 trials made in Chapter 8 of the latter's book *Locomotive Adventure Vol.1*. As it happens I do have the book, but I had not re-acquainted myself with the chapter concerned, prior to writing my critique that you published (*SW36*, p.78).

'Notwithstanding Holcroft's text, I have to advise you that I have not changed my views on the matter at all. If anything, some of the comments made by him in the chapter serve only to reinforce my view – that the inevitable outcome was only to be expected. It was interesting to read that Maunsell approached a number of academics for their views on the matter – I was not aware of this before or the attitude of some of the other drawing office staff to the trial, which hardly surprises me. Having said that, the proof of the pudding is very much in the eating, and the fact that savings could be demonstrated in a stationary plant was clearly enough to convince Holcroft. I am not going to regurgitate any more of Holcroft's comments here but I would urge interested readers to acquaint themselves with the chapter, as it is quite enlightening.

'Please note here, that I did not intend to *criticise* those involved in the A816 trials for trying, but personally I would have thought better of them for their efforts and understanding, as engineers. As I said previously, at the outset of the critique, no doubt "the potential savings were just too irresistible to be ignored", but sometimes you can of course be too close to the wood to be able to see the trees. On balance, Holcroft's contribution to the trials appear to have been inspired by the SHC's consulting engineer but we would after all, expect him to be on top of his game.

'Lastly I would like to put the published record straight here; for the benefit of the *SW* readership and, of course, those who will subsequently read this material. I did not say that Stephenson invented the blast pipe when I explained how he (Stephenson) would have been well aware of its effect on a fire (there would appear to be a number of unaccredited claims for this accolade depending on which author's work you read) and I did not even mention Messrs Kylala, Chapelon, Lemaitre or Giesl in my original critique.

'So for the sake of historical accuracy and to avoid confusing subsequent readers – please let's keeps these matters in their correct context.' *(Chris has submitted some other most interesting pieces. Space alone precludes their inclusion in this issue.)*

Now **to Jim Gosden** and my own comments on steel and No 36001 in the **Editorial to *SW41*.** 'It was interesting to read your comments in the Introduction to *SW41* regarding the email discussion group, Leader No 36001 and its considered failure due to "substandard steel and that this was rife after the Second World War". What arrant nonsense! We must avoid at all costs misinformation which if not tested and questioned will be accepted as historic fact, and that goes for all history.

'To attempt to set the record straight – at nearly 85 years old I can remember the Second World War and its aftermath. If anything there was a shortage of steel for domestic products

No A763, the 'L' class puzzler SECR locomotive referred to earlier by Graham Biggles seen carrying the painted name *Betty Baldwin*. This was inscribed in consequence of the volunteer crews who worked the engine during the 1926 general strike but was painted out in May 1927. *H.C. Casserley*

and projects in the immediate two to three years after the war due to a major effort to re-establish our export markets, especially with regard to the motor and shipbuilding industries. I started my career in mechanical engineering in 1950 and by then there was no shortage of steel, nor was the quality substandard. Common sense and historic fact points to major improvements and development in all forms of steel during the war years to build and replace war weapons, in particular improving armour. Failure to do so would have been utter folly and would have led to defeat in the face of a technically advanced enemy. Those advances continued after the war.

'Additionally our steel industry was privately owned with several large specialised companies scattered across the U.K. and in competition with each other and the USA, so high standards of quality would have continued across the whole range of products from mild steel, high carbon steel and the specialised alloy steels. As you rightly point out, none of Bulleid's other engines suffered similar problems, nor did those built for the other railways.

'If the 'Leader' class was unsuccessful (it certainly was not a failure) it was due if anything to Bulleid ignoring the basic engineering tenet of "KEEP IT SIMPLE", and cramming too many innovations in to the project. Also the lack of interest by the new British Railways engineering hierarchy, which curtailed testing. What is overlooked and not given enough credit is his Turf Burning locomotive in Ireland, which was more successful. Here lessons were learned and put into practice, and Bulleid came very close to moving away from the Stephenson concept, although he retained the reciprocating engine. On the turf burner, the locomotive body could be lifted, the powered bogies rolled out, the compact steam power unit unbolted and a new or reconditioned unit dropped in, not unlike a diesel engine on a lorry. This meant that the time spent out of service would probably been three to four days rather than several weeks for a conventional locomotive.

'Bulleid tends to be remembered today as a brilliant but maverick mechanical engineer verging on a genius. His rightful place in history should be the engineer who mastered the art of locomotive boiler design and built the best locomotive boilers ever seen on Britain's railways, including that for the Leader class. Thanks again for an excellent publication. It never ceases to amaze me at the new and unpublished articles and photographs you find about THE SOUTHERN.' *(Jim, thank you. I might add that, before receiving Jim's note I had made contact with friend and fellow railway author Professor Tony Atkins ('Great Western Wagons'/'Goods Workings' etc), emeritus professor of metallurgy at Reading, who confirmed my own, and subsequently Jim's, views.)*

Finally an appeal from Graham Bowring

'In connection with gathering information for a forthcoming book on the subject, I would like to hear from anyone who has information on LSWR signalling in their own collection. I have been going through many of the well-known sources such as BOT reports, and have access to many official LSWR documents (e.g. old WTT's and some signalling instructions) thanks to help from the South Western Circle and many helpful people, but there are a few gaps as expected. They include for example, photos of the many early boxes which were replaced in major resignalling schemes in the 1890's or after such as Winchester Jct, Alderbury Jct, Hamworthy Jct, Lymington Jct, Virginia Water, Aldershot - Farnham - Alton and many other locations. Also, it would be good to see a few more photos of box interiors; the date of these is not important as long as they show the box with a good amount of original equipment and clearly show the lever frame, and the block shelf with its block instruments and other equipment. Finally, LSWR period box diagrams and photos of more specialised outdoor equipment such as point lock bars and FPL's, point indicators, unusual signals etc. I know all this is rather a long shot and it simply may not exist, but if anyone has anything which they think may be of help and is prepared to share it and / or allow its use in a book, I would be very grateful if they could contact me via the editor.'

Holman Fred Stephens '150'

Ross Shimmon

The Light Railway Empire of
COLONEL H.F. STEPHENS

Weston Point
Welsh Highland Railway ★
Ashover Light Railway ★
Ffestiniog Railway ★
★ Shropshire & Montgomeryshire
★ Snailbeach
★ Edge Hill
Weston, Clevedon & Portishead ★
Burry Port & Gwendreath Valley ★
Sheppey Light ★
HQ, Tonbridge ○
★ East Kent
North Devon & Cornwall ★
Hawkhurst ★
★ Kent & East Sussex
★ Rye & Camber
Selsey Tramway ★
Bere Alston & Callington ★

0   50   100 km

Reproduced from Ordnance Survey map data by permission of Ordnance Survey © Crown copyright 2013

Setting the Scene

Holman Fred Stephens was born on 31 October 1868 – 150 years ago. He built or was associated with sixteen light railways, ranging from the Rye & Camber Tramway, through the Shropshire and Montgomeryshire to the Ffestiniog and Welsh Highland. In addition to the Rye and Camber, the lines that fell within the territory of the Southern Railway were: The Paddock Wood & Cranbrook Railway, the Hundred of Manhood & Selsey Tramway, the Kent & East Sussex Railway, the Sheppey Light Railway, the Bere Alston & Callington branch, the East Kent Light Railway and the North Devon & Cornwall Junction Light Railway. He was also involved, briefly, with the Isle of Wight Central Railway. This account relies heavily on the booklet by Brian Janes, *Colonel Stephens – a Celebration*, published by the Kent & East Sussex Railway, supplemented by other sources listed at the end.

Stephens – a Brief Biography

Stephens was born at a time when railway construction in new areas was coming to an end. Railway companies were consolidating into larger private concerns that survived until the grouping in 1923. Nevertheless, railways still excited the public imagination and his own interest in railways was apparent at an early age.

Stephens was born into a family where art and literature predominated. His father was Frederic G. Stephens, the Pre-Raphaelite artist and critic, examples of whose work were bequeathed by his son to the Tate Gallery. Stephens's godfather was Holman Hunt, best known for his painting *The Light of the World*. He was christened Holman after him. Stephens's educational achievements were noteworthy rather than outstanding. After matriculating in 1887, he briefly studied civil engineering at University College London under Sir Alexander Kennedy. 'Holly' Stephens was then apprenticed at the

Col Stephens Railway Museum Collection

workshops of the Metropolitan Railway in 1881 as a pupil of the Locomotive Superintendent, John Hanbury. In due course, Stephens pressed for an opportunity to gain experience in civils work, his real engineering discipline. Hanbury suggested that he approach Edward P. Seaton, who was working for the Metropolitan on extensive alterations to Baker Street and Portland Road stations – he never hesitated to take advantage of family connections and made play of his family's acquaintance with Sir Edward Watkin, Chairman of both the South Eastern and Metropolitan Railways. This was probably enough to persuade Seaton to take Stephens on. A consulting engineer with twenty years' experience, Seaton was responsible for the design and the route and structures of the Cranbrook and Paddock Wood railway (later the Hawkhurst branch).

Edward P. Seaton employed Stephens as resident engineer for the Hawkhurst line, his first railway project. Still learning, at the relatively tender age of 22, he absorbed many of the distinctive features and materials used in the buildings on this railway and adopted them subsequently on other schemes. He claimed to have had responsibility for sole supervision of the works, including setting out the line. He also resided at Cranbrook throughout the construction period and beyond. The structures of the simpler stations were, in effect, prototypes for those of several other lines in which Stephens had a hand and would became familiar to generations of enthusiasts, several surviving into the heritage era.

The Hawkhurst project was an ideal opportunity for Stephens to gain practical experience. The line was an offshoot of the South Eastern and one of the few schemes of his that involved a major established railway company. After the line was completed in 1893, Stephens stayed on for the customary maintenance period (usually this was one year with railways) and then returned to London with little prospect for immediate work. He had, though, carefully nurtured an acquaintance with Sir Myles Fenton, General Manager of the South Eastern, by sending him tickets for Royal Academy exhibitions and gifts of engravings supplied by his father. He claimed that Sir Myles had virtually promised that, if the proposed extension of the Hawkhurst line to Appledore were to go ahead, he would be given the job of supervising the works, but this line was not to be.

In May 1894, Seaton proposed Stephens for associate membership of the Institute of Civil Engineers. Other distinguished members who put their names on the application include his old tutor, Sir Alexander Kennedy, W. Wainwright (father of Harry Wainwright, who became the locomotive, carriage and wagon superintendent of the SE&CR) and James Stirling. From then on, Stephens was qualified to undertake projects in his own right. Although he probably remained a civil engineer at heart, he developed a whole railway approach and normally had sole engineering responsibility for his projects.

Holman Stephens (in bowler hat) during his apprenticeship with the Metropolitan Railway on the footplate of Met. Railway Beyer Peacock No.20. (Six similar engines were delivered by Beyer Peacock to the LSWR in 1875.) *Col. Stephens Railway Museum Collection*

HFS with party of surveyors for the K&ESR's Headcorn extension outside the White Lion, Tenterden, 1904. HFS is the tall figure near the centre.
Col Stephens Railway Museum Collection

Building a Light Railway Empire

Stephens gained further experience with the construction and success in 1895 of the tiny and cheaply built Rye and Camber Tramway, on which he even advocated using an internal combustion engine-powered railcar. He soon set up a consultancy and was then well placed to take advantage of the demand created by the passing of the 1896 Light Railways Act. This he did with vigour on many projects in the following optimistic years; indeed, his practice had grown to such an extent that in 1900 he had opened his well-known office at 23 Salford Terrace, Tonbridge, where some seventeen to twenty staff were employed for most of the next fifty years.

The concept of light railways was thought of as a method of bringing cheaper transport to rural areas. But, with capital problematic and traffic thin, they would have to be built cheaply for later improvement if and when the expected increase in traffic occurred and more capital could be attracted. Tenterden had been crying out for a railway for many years and Stephens, with his newly acquired expertise, became the catalyst for the creation of the Rother Valley Railway and thence the Kent & East Sussex Railway.

With the success of the Rye, Selsey and Rother Valley schemes, Stephens was wholly committed to promoting and creating light railways. He was responsible for nearly 10% of all orders made under the 1896 Act up to March 1908 (twenty-seven, including extensions of time, of the 311 orders). When it is considered that one-third of statutory light railways were street tramways, his significance to the rural light railways movement becomes obvious. Running them was almost a subsidiary activity until after the First World War.

The enthusiasm for rural light railways did not last very long. By 1920 the concept was effectively dead, but Stephens did not give up. He persisted with several schemes and built them when he could. Stephens himself, though moderately wealthy through inheritance, was not a substantial investor in his companies, although he eventually personally owned the Snailbeach and the Selsey lines. He usually held only enough shares to qualify as a director, if necessary. He earned his income in a variety of ways, initially through surveying, engineering and consultancy fees but increasingly from management fees. His Salford Terrace business was a personal one and all expenses came to be paid through these fees, etc. Many of these fees were paid to him in debentures and he became a substantial holder of such certificates. He was also chairman of the Ffestiniog and Welsh Highland Railways, the Shropshire & Montgomeryshire and the Selsey Tramway for extended periods, but he was not fond of committee work and generally preferred to leave such duties to others, particularly close acquaintances.

Stephens' Railways Within the Territory of the Southern Railway

Paddock Wood & Cranbrook (the Hawkhurst Branch)

Young Holman Fred Stephens was the resident engineer during its construction and some of what became his characteristic station buildings were to be seen on it. It was on this job that he met his long-time colleague and his eventual successor, W.H. Austen. The first section (Paddock Wood, on the South Eastern main line, to Cranbrook) officially opened in September 1892. The final section (Cranbrook to Hawkhurst) came into operation the following year. The line was absorbed by the South Eastern Railway in 1900 and worked by it and its successors until closure in 1961. A goods yard crane from this line is now preserved at Tenterden on the K&ESR.

Rye & Camber Tramway

This was the first fruit of the independent career of Stephens. He, with his lifelong assistant W.H. Austen, planned, built and opened this short 3ft gauge line to carry golfers and holidaymakers over the marshes and dunes for the 2 miles from Rye to Camber. It operated on a shoestring from its opening in 1895 until closure on the day after the Second World War was declared. Used intermittently by the military during the war, it was finally torn up in 1946.

The characteristic station at Golf Links still stands in 2018 and is in the ownership of the golf club. The underframe of one of the two carriages, built by Bagnall's, is in the care of the Colonel Stephens Railway Museum at Tenterden.

Hundred of Manhood and Selsey Tramway

Stephens was the engineer and subsequently manager and, in effect, owner of this line, which did much in the beginning to enhance the holiday resort of Selsey. It was opened in 1897 from Chichester on the LB&SCR coast line, to Selsey and was extended a further mile to Selsey Beach in 1908, but this section fell out of use in 1914. Generally known as the Selsey Tram, this was latterly the most ramshackle of the Stephens' empire. It suffered greatly from road competition after the First World War, falling into bankruptcy in the early 1930s and was closed in 1935. The abutments of the lifting bridge over the Portsmouth & Arundel Canal at Hunston have been restored by canal enthusiasts.

Rother Valley Railway, *later* Kent & East Sussex Railway

This was the quintessential Stephens light railway and is reputed to have been his favourite line. As the Rother Valley Railway, it opened from Robertsbridge on the SE&CR main line to Hastings, to Rolvenden (then named Tenterden) in 1900. An extension to Tenterden proper took place in 1903 and a further longer extension to Headcorn on the Tonbridge to Ashford SE&CR main line occurred in 1905. Built and operated as an independent light railway with new locomotives and stock, expediency and lack of capital forced it to economise in due course by using second-hand stock so beloved of enthusiasts. It served a thoroughly rural area and was initially profitable,

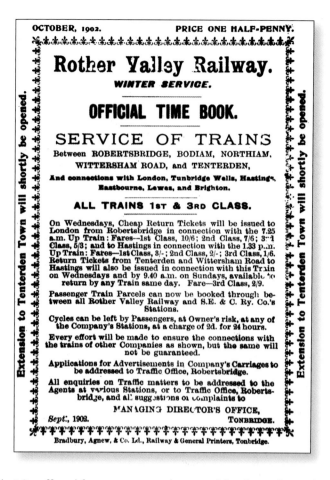

but it suffered from severe road competition from the early 1920s. Only track relaying and imported motive power during the Second Word War and after nationalisation saved it. All passenger traffic ceased at the beginning of 1954 and the railway closed completely in 1961.

Fortunately, enthusiasts rescued the line. Despite much official obstruction in the 1960s, it was progressively reopened from Tenterden in 1974 and reached Bodiam in 2000. Much progress has been made in recent years to complete the section between there and Robertsbridge.

One original locomotive, 'Terrier' No 3 *Bodiam* (ex LBSCR No 70 *Poplar*) survives although it is currently (2018) awaiting overhaul. Several of the stations also survive in more or less original form, whilst many artefacts and paperwork have been preserved for display in the Colonel Stephens Railway Museum.

Sheppey Light Railway

Stephens was the engineer of the Sheppey Light from its inception in 1896 through to opening in 1899: it ran from Queenborough on the SER branch from Sittingbourne to Sheerness (north-south) across the Isle of Sheppey to Leysdown (east-west). Ownership and control passed to the SE&CR in 1905 and then to its successors, in the process losing much of the light railway character, but was still in every way typical of Stephens's construction methods. At first moderately successful, it lost out to electric tram and road competition, closing completely in 1950. Part of the track bed has recently been designated a footpath.

Bere Alston & Callington Branch

The Plymouth, Devonport & South Western Junction Railway promoted this line to join up with and re-gauge the 3ft gauge East Cornwall Mineral Railway to Callington, Stephens was appointed in 1904 to engineer the reconstruction and equip the new line. It opened in 1908 as a light railway under the provision of the Light Railways Act of 1896 with purpose-built locomotives and stock acquired for the opening. Stephens resigned from the railway in 1910. Although closed beyond Gunnislake in 1966, the route from Bere Alston remains open to passenger traffic in 2018. Artefacts and paperwork have been collected and are displayed at Bere Ferrers station.

East Kent Light Railway

Born in great optimism, this railway was the only outcome of numerous plans for railways and collieries in the newly discovered Kent coalfield. Conceived to carry coal, it soon reverted to a rural light railway with a heavy coal flow only for a few miles at one end. Stephens was the engineer from the inception, subsequently becoming a director and manager. Running from Shepherdswell on the SE&CR line from Faversham to Dover, to Wingham with an intermittently operating branch to Richborough Port, it opened in 1911 with a passenger service from 1916. Services ebbed away with the final passenger trains in 1948 and then progressive closures back to Tilmanstone Colliery over the following three years. The colliery shut in the 1980s and the line was closed at the same time. Enthusiasts have since reopened the section from Shepherdswell to Eythorne.

The Isle of Wight Central Railway

Stephens worked with the Isle of Wight Central Railway on two brief occasions. The first commencing in 1904 when the IWCR was interested in acquiring a steam railmotor. The line's manager was instructed to ask Mr Stephens about his experiments [with steam railmotors] but this never came to anything. However, Stephens was appointed engineer to the IWCR in 1911, although the arrangement lasted only a few months. He retired in September of that year, finding that his weekly visits occupied too much of his time. Despite this limited tenure he provided 'umbrella' water tanks at Newport and a Midland Railway six-wheeled travelling crane with match wagon. One of the water tanks survived and is now in use at Havenstreet, the headquarters of the Isle of Wight Steam Railway, while the crane also survived to be taken into the stock of that railway. Remarkably, there is as a result more tangible evidence of his so brief connection with this line than survives of many of the other lines for which he worked longer and harder.

North Devon & Cornwall Junction Light Railway

Reconstructed and considerably extended from a 3ft gauge china clay carrier, this railway was owned by an independent company, but operated by the Southern Railway from its opening in 1925. It was also one of the last standard gauge lines to be built in Britain until HS1.

The 20-mile route ran from Torrington, the then terminus of the ex-LSWR line from Barnstaple, to Halwill Junction, where it met the former LSWR lines to Bude, Padstow and Oakhampton. Colonel Stephens was the engineer and managing director and oversaw its design and construction. The line remained nominally independent until nationalised in 1948, but closed to passengers and partly to goods in 1965. The remaining portion from Torrington to Meeth followed in 1982.

Cutting the first sod of the Halwill-Torrington line, the North Devon & Cornwall Junction Light Railway at Hatherleigh in 1922. Those present include (1) Mr Arthur Neal, MP, Parliamentary Secretary to the Ministry of Transport, who is at work with the spade, (2) Stephens, (3) Mr J. Wilson, formerly Engineer, Great Eastern Railway. H. Montague Bates, chairman of the company, was also present but is not identified. *Col Stephens Railway Museum Collection*

Although not directly 'Southern'-related, a delightful view of Stephens riding in a brake van whilst inspecting works on the Shropshire & Montgomery line.
Col Stephens Railway Museum Collection

Stephens: The Military Man

Stephens was never a full-time army officer, but a member of the 'volunteer forces', (later the Territorials) and was therefore able to continue his railway work in parallel with his military career. He became secretary of the University College School cadet company and in 1888 attended a summer camp at Aldershot at the age of 20. His first commission came in 1896, when he was granted the rank of second-lieutenant with the 1st Sussex (Volunteer) Royal engineers at Eastbourne. He was promoted to captain in 1898 and recruited some 600 men to serve with the Royal Engineers in the Boer War in South Africa. Stephens reached the rank of major, acting as commanding officer of the five companies of the Kent (Fortress) Royal Engineers, moving to his headquarters in Chatham in 1913. In 1916 he was further promoted and had reached the rank of lieutenant colonel. From then on he was known as Colonel Stephens. As the First World War dragged on, Stephens devoted more of his time away from railways to the military effort, whilst the War Department put pressure on him to become full-time in the army. Given an ultimatum of full-time army service or his blossoming railway empire, Stephens returned to Salford Terrace, whilst remaining in the Territorial Force Reserve. It was not until 1925 that Stephens gave up his active military role.

After the Great War

The end of the Great War changed the direction of Stephens's business and increasingly he became less a promoter and builder and more a manager. His Salford Terrace office turned from design and construction to centralised accounting and administration, engineering maintenance and oversight. Nevertheless, Stephens still managed to build the 60cm gauge Ashover Light Railway (which opened in 1924) and, of course, the North Devon & Cornwall Junction. He was much liked and respected by many senior railwaymen, including arguably the best railway manager of his generation, Sir Herbert Walker (who was quite candid about the poor viability of Stephens's lines). Gilbert Szlumper, who was to become Walker's successor, was also a close family friend. Stephens acquired and cultivated a wide circle of such acquaintances, including such worthies as Sir George Barrahell, whom he seems to have met as a senior Treasury official associated with transport issues, and who was later Chairman of Dunlop, |Indeed, Barrahell was his most frequent luncheon companion. He had immense personal charm and wit and was much admired and liked by his staff. His attitude to women was always courteous, sometimes supercilious – occasionally mysterious. He nevertheless had few friends outside his business acquaintances and lived a solitary existence mainly in hotels or at his clubs. Latterly, he was a resident at the Lord Warden Hotel, Dover, where he died on 23 October 1931 aged 62.

Rolvenden yard KESR, 21 September 1931. *H.C. Casserley*

Conclusions

Faced with the problems that Stephens had to confront, many would have gladly given up their independence. There is no doubt he was an optimist who put his private money into these railways. He made a considerable positive contribution to the economies of the areas that his railways served. To start with they were smart efficient concerns within the limitations of their initial construction. Many employed new locomotives and stock. Only when rapid road motor development and the inevitable competition took hold did the need to use second-hand equipment and economies to the service became imperative. Even then, his innovative approaches, notably the use of petrol-driven railmotors, helped to keep services running. Only the lack of capital prevented the use of the next generation of such vehicles.

He used several methods to increase income generation: hay was made from cutting lineside grass and sold on, whilst War Department surplus octagonal huts were set up alongside the Shropshire & Montgomeryshire Railway and advertised as camping huts for hire. Evidence from paperwork recovered from Biddenden station on the K&ESR also suggests the use of vending machines, and advertisements were placed in the press promoting sites suitable for light industries. Stephens was also keen to advertise his lines as providing journeys 'away from dusty roads using British steel rather than imported rubber'. The make-do-and-mend of his last years, together with the perceived need to maintain his balance sheet by not disposing of assets, combined with a probable sentimental attachment to some items, led to the accumulation of obsolete

Shefflex Railmotor complete with baggage car about to be loaded with a pram at Selsey.

and worthless rolling stock that was perhaps misunderstood. It attracted several generations of railway enthusiasts, who recorded with delight ancient steam engines and rolling stock together with railmotors well beyond their prime. Nevertheless, he kept the railways going. Indeed, if any criticism can be directed against Stephens, it is that he failed to anticipate the arrival of the motor lorry and bus and its impact on rural business.

Stephens was, in the last analysis, a man of his time and, like the Light Railways Act so associated with him, was perhaps born too late. We should, however, admire him for his energy and achievement in the circumstances of his heyday and not for the observably crumbling elements of his achievements that were all that was evident to later, and indeed current, generations.

Biographical notes, Sources and Acknowledgments

This article was prepared to mark the 150th anniversary of the birth of Holman F. Stephens. It is almost entirely based on works by Brian Janes, notably, *Colonel Stephens – a Celebration, Kent & East Sussex Railway*, which is available from the railway. Also, the very useful compilation of articles from the *Tenterden Terrier*, the house journal of the Kent & East Sussex Railway, *Colonel Stephens, Insights into the Man and his Empire,* Philip Shaw and Vic Mitchell, Middleton Press, 2005, has been consulted. The latter is, sadly, out of print; a new edition incorporating later research would be welcome in the absence of a biography. The first port of call for anyone seriously interested in Colonel Stephens and his railways must be the Colonel Stephens Railway Museum at Tenterden, Kent. It contains a fascinating collection of exhibits starting with Stephens himself, his parents and childhood home. Separate displays are devoted to each of his lines follow, together others demonstrating aspects of his work. One of the most popular exhibits is *Gazelle*, from the S&MR, currently on loan from the National Railway Museum. Among the outside exhibits is a full-size replica of a Ford railmotor, characteristic of several lines in the Stephens empire. Another rich source of information is the website of the Colonel Stephens Society www.colonelstephenssociety.co.uk. It now incorporates a huge amount of material transferred from the former website of the Colonel Stephens Railway Museum.

The following published works have also been referred to:

The East Kent Railway (2 volumes). M. Lawson Finch & S.R. Garrett, Oakwood Press, 2003.

The Hawkhurst branch. Brian Hart, Wild Swan, 2000.

The Kent & East Sussex Railway. Brian Hart, Wild Swan, nd.

The Rye & Camber Tramway, Laurie A. Cooksey, Plateway Press, 1995.

The Selsey Tramway (2 volumes). Laurie A Cooksey, 2006.

The Sheppey Light Railway. Brian Hart, Wild Swan, 1992.

The Lines and Stations Dr Beeching Did Not Close
Part 2: 1948-1962

Sandling Junction station with 'D3' No 32380 with the branch train for Hythe, 31 August 1949. The train is an Ashford to Hythe pull-push working. Services on this, the truncated branch to Sandgate, ceased from 3 December 1951. Evidence of earlier economy is also visible with the branch having been singled in 1931. *Stephenson Locomotive Society/S.C. Nash*

After the Second World War it appears as if a wave of nostalgia was beginning to recognise railway closures as something to be noted. As an example of this we may take the closing of the Sheppey Light Railway (Leysdown to Queenborough) from Monday 4 December 1950, which was reported in newspapers of the previous day.

The *Daily Mail* quoted as follows under the heading 'Man Rides 50 Miles to Hear Last Puff': 'Michael Spellen, 28 year old electrician, cycled for miles to see locomotive 31705 puff across the Isle of Sheppey for the last time. Other railway enthusiasts came from all over the country. British Railways has struck the 50-year-old Sheppey Light Railway off the operational map because it has not paid its way for years. No 31705's route was seven miles long – from Leysdown to Queenborough. Yesterday the Sheppey Light Railway was silent. The last trip was on Saturday night. The two coaches were crammed. At Leysdown station a procession of mourners in top hats and frock-tail coats carried a coffin draped in black. It bore the inscription 'R.I.P. to dear old Sheppey Light Railway – no more to trip through tulips. The coffin was laid in the luggage van, a wreath was put on the buffers and 31705 set out. Bells clanged, hooters blasted, whistles shrieked, and big drums beat as the old train rumbled along the single line. At all the halts villagers swarmed round the engine and said goodbye to 50-year-old driver Tom Birchwell and his young fireman Don Pilcher, both of Sittingbourne.

Another funeral procession of locals in top hats and frock-tail coats waited at Minster-on-Sea. They carried a coffin and a wreath made of cabbage leaves and onions: "To the memory of the Sheppey Light Railway, so dear to us all". They laid them in the guard's van. All along the line, men, women and children flung open the windows to wave goodbye. At Queenborough the coffins were unloaded, heads were bared, and the Last Post sounded by trumpeters. Mr Spellen had cycled from Elm Close, Croydon. He said, "I wouldn't have missed this for anything."

Lines closed 1948 to 1962:

Entries in italics refer to lines absorbed into or transferred by boundary changes into Southern Region control.

Eastry–Shepherds Well	1 November 1948
Eastr–Wingham	1 November 1948
Leysdown–Queenborough	4 December 1950
Port Victoria–Grain Crossing Halt	11 June 1951
Hythe–Sandling Junction	3 December 1951
Easton–Melcombe Regis	3 March 1952
Bulford–Porton (Amesbury Junction)	30 June 1952
Newton Tony–Grateley	30 June 1952
Brookwood–Bisley Camp	21 July 1952
Merstone–Ventnor West	15 September 1952
Canterbury–Whitstable (to goods)	1 December 1952
Fareham–Gosport	8 June 1953
Gravesend West–Farningham Road (Fawkham Junction)	3 August 1953
Brading–Bembridge	21 September 1953
Newport–Freshwater	21 September 1953
Headcorn–Robertsbridge	4 January 1954
Nunhead–Crystal Palace HL	20 September 1954
Alton–Fareham (Meon Valley line) (to passengers)	7 February 1955
(Section Droxford to Farringdon closed completely)	
Petersfield–Pulborough (to passengers)	7 February 1955
(Section Petersfield–Midhurst closed completely)	
Edenbridge (Crowhurst Junction north–south)	13 June 1955
East Grinstead–Lewes (Culver Junction)	15 June 1955
(Last train was 29 May 1955. Line reopened 7 August 1956)	
Ludgershall–Tidworth	19 September 1955
Newport–Sandown	6 February 1956
Bentley–Bordon	16 September 1957
East Grinstead–Lewes (Culver Junction)	17 March 1958
Melcombe Regis–Weymouth Junction	14 September 1959
Newbury (Enborne Junction)–Shawford Junction (to passengers)	7 March 1960
Barnstaple Victoria Road–South Loop Junction	13 June 1960
Westerham–Dunton Green	30 October 1961
Allhallows-on-Sea–Gravesend Central (Hoo Junction)	4 December 1961
Grain–Gravesend Central (Hoo Junction)	4 December 1961
Allhallows-on-Sea–Stoke Junction Halt	4 December 1961
Hawkhurst–Paddock Wood	12 June 1961

'Mr Peter Walker of Birmingham, a member of the Light Railway League, travelled 160 miles. He said, "This is a melancholy event, but my friends and I had to be here." And Mr David Cheney of Rugby, who came 130 miles said, "This is an historic occasion and a sad one to those of us who enthuse about light railways." Driver Tom nodded and said, "The old Sheppey line has been a friend to thousands. Now she is gone."'

Another newspaper carried a similar report, adding that one of the passengers was 71-year-old Jack Buddle, who had driven the first train in 1901. Due also to an improved, and likely more convenient, bus service, takings for the line had been reduced to 'a paltry few shillings daily'.

The then terminus at Hythe with pull-push set No 652 ready to be pulled back to Sandling Junction, 1 November 1951. On the final day of service, Saturday, 1 December, a clean member of the 'C' class, No 31721, bedecked with a wreath was noted on the last train at Hythe.
Stephenson Locomotive Society/S.C. Nash

With just four weeks of life left, 'T9' No 30719 will hardly be taxed with a single van at Bulford on 2 June 1952 – services ending on 30 June. Built very much with the military in mind, the route to Amesbury and Bulford saw considerable use in wartime but with a return to peace it could hardly pay its way. Notwithstanding public closure, military specials continued to operate for several years with the line not finally closing to all traffic until March 1963.
Stephenson Locomotive Society/S.C. Nash

With five years of passenger service still remaining, 'M7' No 30328 leaves Selham with the 11.27am Petersfield to Pulborough train on 15 October 1950. *Stephenson Locomotive Society/S.C. Nash*

A single coach suffices for this Kent & East Sussex Railway train seen at Robertsbridge. Services over the complete length of the KESR ceased from 4 January 1954. In charge is 'Terrier' No 32678 that, together with sister engine No 32655, was later responsible for working the last train over the line. Both engines are now preserved. *Stephenson Locomotive Society/S.C. Nash*

Carriage roof board especially prepared for the very last passenger working over the full Midhurst and Meon Valley lines, Sunday, 6 February 1955. Definitely also a case of said roof board having a single use! There was no Sunday service over either route and consequently the last public passenger trains had operated on the Saturday.
Stephenson Locomotive Society/S.C. Nash

Photographing the photographers! The scene at Midhurst years later with the arrival of the very last passenger train – a special working – and which coincided with complete closure of the railway in 1964. Of note must be the change in fashions from that time. *A. Hemens*

Demolition at West Hoathley on 21 October 1960. 'K' class 2-6-0 No 32353 assisting with track recovery. *Stephenson Locomotive Society/S.C. Nash*

With due acknowledgement to Anthony Hemens, the Stephenson Locomotive Society and in particular Gerry Nichols. Likewise the Transport Treasury and in particular Robin Fell. Reference also made to:

A History of the Southern Railway by C.F. Dendy Marshall (Ian Allan, 1963).

Passengers No More by G. Daniels and L.A. Dench (Ian Allan, 1980).

Article on the internet by J.S. Dodgson www.bath.ac.uk/e-journals/jtep/pdf/ Volume_XV111_No_3_219-235.pdf

Opposite top: **Last public day at Bordon, Saturday, 14 September 1957. 'M7' No 30110 has charge of the 12.47pm pull-push working from Bordon. Other than the cameraman there would appear to be one other photographer present.** *Stephenson Locomotive Society/S.C. Nash*

Bottom: **BR Class 4 No 80016 paused at Sheffield Park with the 12.03pm through train from Victoria to Brighton on 16 April 1955. At this time, closure had already been agreed consequent upon British Railways' own branch line report. This was scheduled to take effect from 15 June, but in the event the last train ran on 29 May due to a nationwide ASLEF dispute. However, it was not to be the end as local (Chailey) resident Margery Bessemer discovered the closure had contravened the original Act of Parliament relating to the railway and BR had no choice but to reinstate services from 7 August 1956. It was to be a short-lived reprieve and, following a public enquiry and the necessary action by Parliament, the route was finally closed – at the time considered for good – from 17 March 1958.**

The branch train at Westerham on 11 April 1952, the service being the 1.28pm to Dunton Green with 'R1' No 31704 at the head. Westerham was a branch line destined to become infamous so far as a political rail closure was concerned. Suffice to say, opposition was considerable especially as the Transport Consultative Committee argued that in excess of 200 passengers were using the line daily. A number of underhand meetings were also hinted at but in the end the pessimists won through with the last passenger trains running at the end of October 1961. Today part of the route is under the M25 motorway. (The full story of the Westerham Branch is told in the book of the same name, written by Ron Strutt and due to be published by Crecy Publishing in 2018. *Stephenson Locomotive Society/S.C. Nash*

As has been discussed in recent issues of *SW*, the use of the ACV diesel set in Kent had until recently (or so we thought) escaped the camera. Here though is another image of the unit, seen at Gravesend Central with an Allhallows train, likely on 31 March 1961. *Stephenson Locomotive Society/S.C. Nash*

The Low-Pressure Pneumatic Signalling System
A Brief History
John Wagstaff via Michael Upton

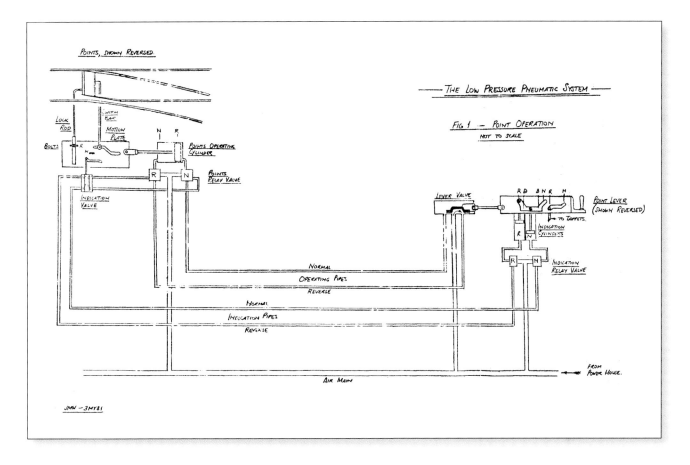

Point operation – LPP. The sketch at Fig. 1 shows the operation of a single set of points by this system. The switches are shown to be lying in the reverse position, and the method of replacing these to normal is as described next.

During the last two decades of the nineteenth century, signal engineers in Europe and America devoted much attention to the possibility of the operation by power of signals and points. The initial advantage to be gained from this was the ability to work signals a considerable distance from a lever frame, but an additional benefit, not at first recognised, was the possibility of working signals automatically, without the physical labour of a signalman.

The first practical automatic signals in Great Britain were those fixed on the Liverpool Overhead Railway in 1893, but these did not use track circuits, and were operated by striker-boards fitted to the rear of each train, which engaged mechanical treadles fixed by the side of the track.

Nothing more was done with automatic signalling until the autumn of 1900, when a visit was paid to the United States by two officers of the London and South-Western Railway, Mr Jacomb Hood, the chief engineer, and Mr Sam Fay, then superintendent of that line and later general manager of the Great Central Railway.

As a result, a power plant was laid down for working the points and signals at Grateley by the Low-Pressure Pneumatic System, and the 6 miles of double line between Grateley and Andover were equipped with automatic signals on the LPP principle, operated by power generated at the source of supply at Grateley. This was opened in the summer of 1901.

The success of this early installation was sufficient to justify its extension to Woking and Basingstoke. On this section there were four lines and all the points and signals at the stations and junctions were worked by power on the Low-Pressure system, with automatic signals for dividing the intermediate lengths into sections of about 1,500 yards each.

Elsewhere, other railways were experimenting with 'modern' equipment, including on the Great Central Railway where automatic signals on the same system were provided for breaking the long section between Whetstone and Ashby Magna, also for dividing the block section on the Up Line through Woodhead Tunnel. Nearer to home on the Great Western Railway, the section of the four main lines between Pangbourne and Goring, 21 miles, was equipped with automatic signals and track circuits, which were brought into use in August 1907.

By the end of 1910, the LSWR had a total of twenty-four LPP frames in use, with a total of 892 levers on the Low-Pressure system whilst the total in Great Britain at that time had reached 1,740 levers.

Point Operation

The LPP lever frame consists of a row of slides, each having a vertical handle about 4ft in length, and each slide is pierced with a number of cam slots. The slot nearest to the lever handle is used to drive a roller, which operates conventional tappet interlocking. The second slot in the plate contains two rollers, each attached to an Indication Cylinder. At the back of the frame is a valve, which is used to control the points.

In order to place the points to the normal position, the lever handle in the frame is pushed forward a distance of about 2ft, and as this is done the operating bar actuates the interlocking by means of the rod connected to the tappets. The mechanical interlocking is then in neither the normal nor the reverse position, thereby preventing the operation of any signals leading over these points. At the same time, the lever valve will connect the Air Main to the Normal Operating Pipe, feeding air at the reduced pressure of 7lb to the normal side of the Points Relay Valve. The relay valve operates in a manner very similar to an electro-mechanical signalling relay, as in use today; that is, the supply of air via the operating pipe to a relay valve will then connect the air main to the normal side of the Points Operating Cylinder, admitting air at 15lb pressure to the cylinder. The piston pushes the Motion Plate from right to left, and a pin in the switch-bar travelling along the slot draws the points over, so that they move to the normal position.

The initial movement of the motion plate, however, produces no effect upon the switch-bar. This motion disengages the reverse bolt from the Lock Rod, the middle portion of the movement of the motion plate moves the switches, and the final part of the motion locks the points in their new position with the normal bolt. The notches in the locking bar are

Figure 2. Here is shown the arrangement of a stop and distant signal, the down-rods being contained within the tubular post. At the foot of the signal post is a large chamber, illustrated in Fig. 3, on the outside wall of which is fixed a large diaphragm. The supply of air through the operating pipe to the Relay Valve, also contained within the mechanism chamber, will connect the air main to the outside face of this diaphragm, this operating a short rod on the end of which is a roller, and this in turn moving a crank that works the down rod, lowering the signal. The signal is replaced in the manner usual with semaphore signals, by the weight of the spectacle.

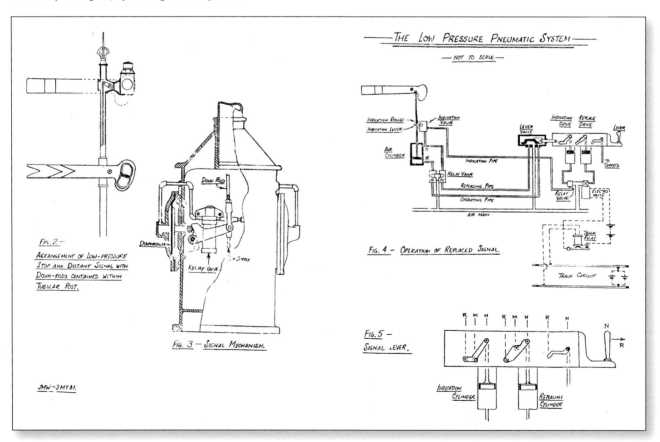

differently cut, so that the reverse and normal bolts can enter only their correct notch. When the motion plate has completed its travel, the Indication Valve allows air to pass through the Normal Indication Pipe to the normal side of the Indication Relay Valve. When the lever handle was pushed forward originally, as described above, the roller attached to the Normal Indication Cylinder prevented the lever moving beyond the (B) position, coming up against an angle in the slot in the lever plate. Admission of air to the normal side of the Indication Relay Valve connects the air main to the normal Indication Cylinder, forcing the piston upwards and completing the stroke from (B) to (N) of the lever. This frees the interlocking, and so allows the corresponding signal lever to be used.

Signal Mechanism

The operation of signals, as shown in the diagram, is very similar to that of points, except that there is no 'Return Indication' for the 'off' position, the indication only being given for the signal when 'on'.

The majority of the signals are replaced automatically by occupation of a track circuit. This is done by automatically replacing the lever itself and making the lever restore the signal. When a train enters the track circuit, the Track Relay is de-energised, and cuts off the feed to the Electro Valve. When this valve is de-energised air is allowed to pass from the main pipe to a replacing cylinder. When the signal lever

The original 1902, sixty-four-lever frame in Salisbury West, recorded by Roger Holmes sometime in the autumn of 1968. The levers (more accurately slides) are coloured to correspond to conventional practice: red – stop signals; blue – locks; black – turnouts (points). Do we dare hazard a guess how many times each might have been pulled/pushed in its seventy-nine-year lifetime? Inspection covers are fitted front and top whilst the block shelf contains a standard SR 3-position block for working to Wilton and a similar standard GWR '1947' block for the connection to and from the 'other railway'. (Was the working between the 'West' and 'East' boxes by track-circuit block as there is no corresponding block-instrument at the far end of the shelf?) Each lever is numbered with the description and the appropriate lever leads (indicating what levers need to be pulled before that specific lever will respond), placed horizontally beneath.

is pulled, the roller associated with the piston of the replacing cylinder is forced to the bottom of the slot in the lever plate, and when air is admitted to the cylinder the piston is raised and this causes a left to right motion of the slide, but only for two-thirds of the travel. This acts in a similar way to the operations of the signalmen replacing the lever, and the air main is connected through the replacing pipe to the normal relay valve.

When the arm has returned fully to normal, the indication roller on the down rod will operate the indication lever, admitting air to the indication pipe, and via a relay valve, forcing upwards the piston in the indication cylinder. This completes the return to normal of the signal lever.

It will be noticed that in this description of a replaced signal, the arm is shown to be operated by an air cylinder. In the Salisbury area, although originally all signals were fitted with a diaphragm mechanism, the majority (if not all) were later modernised, and equipped with air cylinders.

Several other features, unique at the time although commonplace today, were applied in these early installations; automatic working at intermediate stations was common, and the operation of two or more signals from a single lever presented no difficulties. It is believed that the installation at Salisbury was the last mechanically operated power installation in the country, with both the East and West power boxes taken out of use in August 1981.

A close-up of a small portion of the frame – clearly also a quiet time with no trains due to arrive from the west. Notice the bell tapper for 'Salisbury East' at the end of the block shelf and behind a glimpse of a signalman's duster. A pity perhaps that some of the brass plates have been replaced with ivorine labels but times change and where there is brasswork it is clearly still lovingly polished. In each of these two images emergency oil lamps will be noted, although the one seen here is missing its glass funnel.

Accident at Aldershot
9 November 1901
Submitted by Martin Burrell

From *The Aldershot News*, 'Killed in the Fog – Engine Driver's Sudden Fate'

During the heavy fog of Sunday morning a fatal accident occurred, on the South Eastern and Chatham Railway, about a quarter of a mile on the Reading side of Blackwater Station. The victim was Jesse Brant, aged thirty-six years, the driver of a goods train, and a man of the steadiest habits. He leaves a widow and several children. The sadness of his sudden death is the more noticeable inasmuch as it occurred while he was endeavouring to prevent what might have been a catastrophe. While engaged in shunting at Blackwater Station he threw some red hot clinkers out into the six-foot way, and one of these set a sleeper on fire. Brant saw the blaze, shouted to the fireman, and jumped off his engine with a shovel to beat out the flame. At that moment a passenger train from Reading to Redhill came through the fog, almost noiselessly, for steam had been shut off some distance away. Brant was evidently caught completely by surprise and struck by the buffer on the head. The blow killed him instantly.

The remains were taken to the White Hart Hotel, close by Blackwater Station, and there on Tuesday the Deputy Coroner, Mr W.E. Foster, held an inquest. Mr Windsor, Locomotive foreman, Reading attended on behalf of the railway company, and Mr J. Dobson on behalf of the Amalgamated Society of Railway Servants.

The Fireman's Evidence

Arthur John Coleman, who had been seven months working as fireman to the deceased on the Reading Branch, was with him on the engine, of which Brant had charge, at Blackwater at the time of the accident. He stated that they commenced work overnight on Saturday about 8.15pm at Bricklayers Arms, and on Sunday morning were with the down goods train. When they reached Blackwater there was shunting to be done and the engine was so engaged for about an hour before the accident. At that time they were on the down metals, and deceased was throwing clinkers out of the fire into the six-foot way. This was really witness's duty, but it was not an uncommon thing for a driver when he found himself at leisure, to assist the fireman in this way. It was not often that it was necessary to clear out clinkers on a journey; the quality of the coal and the amount of work to be done affected the quantity of clinkers formed. They formed more readily during shunting than during ordinary running. After the clinkers had been thrown out, the engine was shunted back, and in returning, as it arrived at a point about a quarter-mile from the down end of the down platform deceased noticed that a sleeper on the up line had been set on fire. He drew witness's attention to this and jumped off his engine, which was then slowing down, and stopped within the length of two or three trucks. Almost immediately afterwards the up passenger train from Reading passed. This was about a quarter to seven in the morning, it was light, but there was a dense fog, in consequence of which witness had not seen the Reading train approaching. Had it not been for the fog it would have been quite possible to have noticed the train coming.

Witness heard the passenger train putting on the brake, and surmised something had happened to deceased. He afterwards saw Brant's body lying in the six-foot way. Life was extinct, but the body remained till it was seen by the doctor and was then removed to the White Hart Hotel.

No Fog Signals

Replying to the Forman Mr Miller, witness said the shunting was being done between two up signals, but as the engine had the whole down line to itself he personally paid no attention to the up signals. Deceased had apparently forgotten that the up train was about due.

Asked by Mr Dobson how it was that after the clinkers had been cleared out at Bricklayers Arms they should again require to be removed before arriving at Reading, witness said his firebox was smaller than some and it had been leaking between London and Redhill. The quality of the coal might also account for it.

Witness stated, in answer to other questions, that the only other place where they had done much shunting that morning was at Betchworth. Deceased had been working on the Reading Branch for about twenty years.

John Edwards, the driver of the up train, said he had been thirty-eight years a driver on the Reading Branch. He knew deceased well and last saw him about a week ago, deceased hearing was good, and he was a steady man and a careful driver. Witness had not noticed deceased's engine till he was close upon it, in consequence of the fog, which made it almost impossible to see beyond the chimney of the engine. The gradient from Wellington College was down and witness had shut off steam as usual, about a mile from Blackwater Station, he would therefore be proceeding almost noiselessly. If on the other hand deceased had just put the brake on his own engine, there would be a good deal of creaking and noise among the trucks of the goods train as it came to a standstill. Witness had frequently cleaned out clinkers from his own firebox, though it was probably the fireman's duty, they ought not to require to be turned out during a run, but it would sometimes happen, and witness had known sleepers to be set alight in this way, had he been in the deceased place he would probably have acted just as he had done. It was not part of the deceased's duty to study the up signal, and in fact, they could not be seen except from just below them. There were no fog signals out this morning, and if there had been any, they would not go off unless to show that the road was blocked. It was not customary on the South Eastern and Chatham Railway to have fog signals that went off simply to show that a signal had been passed.

In answer to the foreman, witness said he had not begun to whistle, as he was too far from the station. Had there been a fog signal by the distant signal, deceased might have heard it, engine driver felt a shock. Further questioned by the coroner, witness said he felt a shock of something touching the engine, and looking down at once saw deceased flung aside, he put on the brakes, and sent the fireman to tell the signalman why he had pulled up, afterwards he went himself to see the body, in which there was no life left. Walter Drew the fireman on the passenger train gave evidence corroborative of the driver's statements.

Dr Denny, who viewed the body, was unable to attend, but Dr J.I. Adams described the injuries as fracture of the base of the skull, or of the junction of the skull and the spine. Death he said must have been instantaneous from the appearance of the injury deceased had been stooping down and had time simply to throw up his head, which was struck by the buffer of the engine.

In summing up, the coroner said that probably ninety-nine men out of a hundred would have acted as deceased did in trying to put out the fire even if it were against any number of regulations. He expressed sympathy with the widow and orphans, but considered the affair one of those unavoidable accidents to which railway servants were especially liable.

At the request of a juryman, the room was cleared while they considered their verdict, which was eventually brought in as 'accidental death' they absolved deceased from all blame, and directed the coroner to write to the railway company, urging them to have fog signals on days like Sunday. They wished the company to be reminded that some years ago, a porter was killed while opening the level crossing gates in a fog, and that a recommendation for the use of fog signals was made by the Coroner jury at that time."

Editor's note: This is another example where no formal investigation appears to have been carried out by the Board of Trade (then the investigating authority for railway accidents). That is not to say there was not likely to have been a railway enquiry but it would be very interesting to know what criteria was applied as to when an accident (or other incident) warranted a formal investigation.

Southern EMUs

I have been called to task on more than one occasion in the past for seeming to concentrate on steam when the Southern was also the operator of by far the largest suburban electric system in England. Valid criticism indeed but with the excuse that material on (historic) EMUs is often conspicuous by its very absence and so it was with some feelings of relief that we were recently given access to the small collection of images that follow.

Possibly one of the reasons for this lack of material was that to many the humble EMU was seen as little more than a means of conveyance, a 'set of boxes on wheels' to be endured rather than enjoyed. And yet whilst that may be the subjective view of some, who cannot say that the 'City', 'Pul', 'Pan' and 'Cor' sets (including the latter's derivatives) were not without their own charm? Of course, years on we may hanker back to

those stifling days in a 6-aside 'Sub', or the whining pitch of a 'Bil' as it accelerated between stops, but remember too the constricting and frantic attempt to alight at one's stop trying to avoid, feet, bags and umbrellas. This was made ever more difficult if the train had already stopped or slowed several times and it was a day when the inside of the windows were already running with condensation, so making it difficult to identify each particular stopping place. There was also a sort of soporific charm at being compressed between one's fellow travellers, especially when the heating was on, and in consequence on many occasions a passenger might find himself carried some way beyond his intended destination. Thus, for no other reason than a genuine attempt to appease certain detractors, I sincerely hope you enjoy what follows.

We start in the late 1930s, 9 July 1937 to be precise, with this recorded image of a '10 Bel' set working the 3.00pm Victoria to Brighton, the 'Brighton Belle' of course, just about to pass Clapham Junction on the down run. For the record the sets are Nos 3053 and 3051.

A second Clapham Junction view, this time taken a couple of months earlier on 27 May 1937, but as may be determined from the '4' headcode, another Victoria to Brighton service. On this occasion it is a single six-car set, '6Pul' No 3019 and which was originally allocated Pullman car 'Peggy' in its formation.

London termini, with another '6Pul', this time No 3008 just departing. Unfortunately it is not possible to read the roofboards. Two points on this image, the first in reference to the coupling at the end of the coach, of the standard screw type. Regular readers might care to remember this with regard to an incident that will be illustrated in the Stephen Townroe section of the next issue, *SW44* (we will say no more for now). Secondly, the obvious point of the driver having an enviable clear view ahead, certainly better than nearly every steam engine – excepting No 36001, of course. But years later, in the 1950s, BR were concerned that for main-line work a driver might well become distracted, nay even memorised, by the supposed 'strobe' effect of sleepers flashing past at speed. When mention was made that the drivers of Southern EMUs had satisfactorily dealt with this issue for years, the answer was ignored or reduced to the 'that is only slow speed suburban working'. Clearly somebody had conveniently forgotten the Eastbourne, Brighton and Portsmouth line services. No specific date is given, although we are told this is also 1937.

To a more rural environment now with the 12 noon up, Ore and Eastbourne to Victoria service at Lewes on 15 July 1937. This is set No 3013, probably with *Brenda* as the Pullman. From the image one can almost feel the rocking motion, particularly noticeable on the third and fourth vehicles, as the train negotiates the trackwork. In Southern days post-1939, headcode '50' was changed to indicate a Victoria to Littlehampton working.

On 6 August 1937, '6Cit' No 3043 and an unidentified '6Pan' had charge of the 5.00pm 'City Limited' from London Bridge to Brighton, the train seen at East Croydon. This working had a limited operational life, being withdrawn at the start of the Second World War and not reinstated with a return to peace, the former '6Cit' sets subsequently re-formed into '6Pul' units.

Oppsite top: Modern traction near to Bedhampton Halt between Havant and Fratton comprising two '2Bil' sets, Nos 2045 and 2034. The view was taken on 3 July 1937, just one day before the inauguration of electrification on the 'Portsmouth Direct', and is also reported as the 1.57pm stopping service from Waterloo to Portsmouth & Southsea. Assuming this information to be correct, and the 'No 7' headcode does indeed refer to such a working, then this would indicate that some services at least had been turned over to electric working in advance of the formal commencement.

Bottom: We move now almost twenty years forward to the mid-1950s and some views of EMUs around the suburban system. Little caption information was provided by the photographer, other than we are told this is a down service at the station shown, Charlton, on 12 July 1956. '4Epb' set No 5159 is in charge and still displaying the 'S' prefix. On the opposite platform are a number of examples of the products of Exmouth Junction.

Slightly earlier in time, on a sunny 8 August 1953, we have another view of Charlton, this time from the footbridge looking down on to an up train of mixed vintage. From the position of the starting signal we can glean this service was due to travel towards Maze Hill and Deptford.

Another '4Epb', this time No 5113 at Maze Hill on 12 July 1955, and where again platform work is under way. Of just as much interest are the various coach sets on the left, sets 898 and 389 being identified. Headcode '81' was used for three different workings: Cannon Street to Dartford via Greenwich; Holborn Viaduct to Swanley or Sevenoaks via Herne Hill, and further afield, Strood to Ramsgate.

We move now to the wooden platforms of Lordship Lane as '4Sub' No 4107 arrives watched by just a handful of potential passengers on 18 September 1954. Two days after the view was taken the station permanently closed, together with the line from Nunhead to Crystal Palace High Level. This was not in fact the first closure, as temporary closures had occurred between 1917 and 1919 and again from 1944 to 1946. This time though there would be no reprieve and the station site is now occupied by a residential estate.

The interior of a deserted Crystal Palace High Level station on 23 May 1953, yet still at the time open to passengers. As mentioned in the previous view, this station closed the following year. Following closure, the station remained abandoned and was not finally demolished until 1961. According to local legend going back to the 1930s, there is the story of a train entombed in a collapsed tunnel nearby and this referenced the 1860s abandoned atmospheric railway on the north side of the park. An archeological dig in the 1970s failed to find any trace.

Chaos at London Bridge (low level) on the morning of 6 April 1957, the day after the Cannon Street signal box fire. Three 'sub' sets lead the line-up of services working a shuttle service, although we not told how accurate the trains' designations may actually be in consequence.

Another '4Sub', possibly No 4651, climbing towards Sutton West Junction and watched by a group of p/way men.

We conclude this piece with a view of a '4Lav' set, No 2940, viewed from a down train approaching the old station at Gatwick Airport. Notice in the six-foot between the up and down running lines, the bin of chippings – used by the p/way department when just slight packing was required. On the up side too new concrete troughing has been offlo--aded and awaits laying.

The
Southern Way

The regular volume for the Southern devotee

MOST RECENT BACK ISSUES

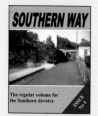

The Southern Way is available from all good book sellers, or in case of difficulty, direct from the publisher. (Post free UK) Each regular issue contains at least 96 pages including colour content.

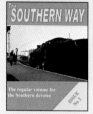

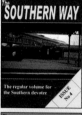

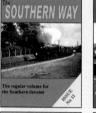

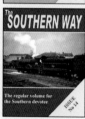

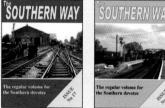
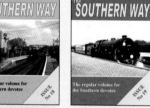

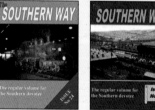

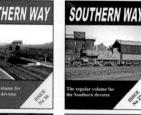

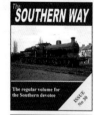

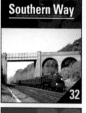
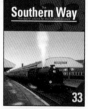
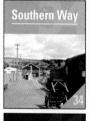
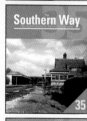

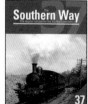
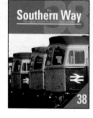
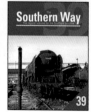
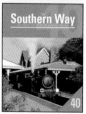
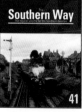
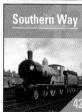

£11.95 each
£12.95 from Issue 7
£14.50 from Issue 21
£14.95 from Issue 35

Subscription for four-issues available
(Post free in the UK)
www.crecy.co.uk